A2 Government & Politics

The US Supreme Court

Anthony J. Bennett

Advanced TopicMaster

Series editor
Eric Magee

Philip Allan Updates, an imprint of Hodder Education, an Hachette UK company, Market Place, Deddington, Oxfordshire OX15 0SE

Orders

Bookpoint Ltd, 130 Milton Park, Abingdon, Oxfordshire OX14 4SB
tel: 01235 827827
fax: 01235 400401
e-mail: education@bookpoint.co.uk
Lines are open 9.00 a.m.–5.00 p.m., Monday to Saturday, with a 24-hour message answering service. You can also order through the Philip Allan Updates website: www.philipallan.co.uk

© Anthony J. Bennett 2010

ISBN 978-0-340-98722-3

First printed 2010
Impression number 5 4 3 2 1
Year 2014 2013 2012 2011 2010

Printed in Spain

Hachette UK's policy is to use papers that are natural, renewable and recyclable products and made from wood grown in sustainable forests. The logging and manufacturing processes are expected to conform to the environmental regulations of the country of origin.

P01750

Contents

Contents

Introduction

Standing just across the road from the Capitol in Washington DC is the imposing building of the United States Supreme Court. Carved on the architrave of the west facade is the text: 'Equal Justice Under Law'. Less often seen — on the east side of the building — is another text: 'Justice the Guardian of Liberty'. In this volume, the third in a series on the three branches of the federal government, we consider issues of law and liberty. The members of the Supreme Court are not as high-profile as the president or even congressional leaders. I suspect most Americans could pass by members of the Court in the street without recognising them. In the summer of 2004, I happened to meet the then Chief Justice, William Rehnquist, in the dining room of the Swan Hotel in Lavenham, Suffolk. He was staggered to be recognised.

The questions to be answered

As in previous volumes, we address six key questions. We start with the nomination and confirmation process: what is wrong with it and how could it be improved? We then consider the extent to which a president can influence the political balance of the Court. This proves to be more difficult for a president to do than is genuinely believed. In the third chapter we ask the question, 'Can the Supreme Court "amend" the US Constitution?' Of course in the literal sense it cannot, but through its power of judicial review, it can change the *meaning* of the Constitution, making, as it were, interpretive amendments. In this chapter, we also consider the debate between those justices who describe themselves as 'originalists' and those who believe in a 'living Constitution'. In Chapter 4, we debate whether or not the Supreme Court has effectively protected the rights and liberties of US citizens. This is a complex issue, for society's views on what constitute the accepted rights and liberties of citizens has changed significantly over the decades — let alone the centuries. We consider three areas of rights and liberties — those concerning race, abortion and freedom of religion. 'Is the US Supreme Court a political institution?' is the question addressed in Chapter 5. Its members are appointed by a politician and confirmed by politicians, and it makes judgements which have profound political significance. After all, in 2000 it virtually decided the result of the presidential election — surely it must be political. Finally, we ask whether Supreme Court justices should still be appointed for life. If not, what about some alternatives — fixed terms, a mandatory retirement age or election?

1 What is wrong with how justices are chosen?

On 9 April 2010, Supreme Court Justice John Paul Stevens wrote a brief letter to President Obama. It read simply:

> My dear Mr President:
>
> Having concluded that it would be in the best interests of the Court to have my successor confirmed well in advance of the commencement of the Court's next Term, I shall retire from regular active service as an Associate Justice effective the next day after the Court rises for the summer recess this year.
>
> Most respectfully yours,
>
> John Paul Stevens

This letter set in motion the process whereby President Obama would choose a successor to Justice Stevens, one which resulted in the nomination and confirmation of Justice Elena Kagan. Vacancies to the nine-member Supreme Court occur, on average, every 2 or so years. Thus a one-term president might expect to make one or possibly two appointments to the Court, whilst a two-term president might make three or even four appointments. One-term president George H. W. Bush (1989–93) made two nominations to the Court; two-term president Ronald Reagan (1981–89) made three, plus the promotion of William Rehnquist from being an associate justice to chief justice. But it does not always work out that way. Jimmy Carter (1977–81) made no appointments at all and both Bill Clinton (1993–2001) and George W. Bush (2001–09) made only two appointments in each of their 8-year periods. As Supreme Court justices enjoy life tenure, a vacancy occurs only when a justice resigns, retires or dies. In the 35 years between 1975 and 2010, there were just 13 vacancies on the Court — eleven as a result of retirements, one as a result of the promotion of an associate justice to chief justice, and one as a result of a death (see Table 1.1).

There has of late been a good deal of criticism about the nomination and confirmation process for Supreme Court justices. But this is pretty much focused on the events of the last 25 years or so. Have things always been this bad and if not, why not? What were the intentions of the Founding Fathers

Table 1.1 Supreme Court vacancies: 1975–2010

Date	President	Justice causing vacancy	Reason for vacancy	Replaced by
1975	Gerald Ford	William Douglas	Retired	John Paul Stevens
1981	Ronald Reagan	Potter Stewart	Retired	Sandra Day O'Connor
1986	Ronald Reagan	Warren Burger	Retired	William Rehnquist
1986	Ronald Reagan	William Rehnquist	Promoted	Antonin Scalia
1987	Ronald Reagan	Lewis Powell	Retired	Anthony Kennedy
1990	George H. W. Bush	William Brennan	Retired	David Souter
1991	George H. W. Bush	Thurgood Marshall	Retired	Clarence Thomas
1993	Bill Clinton	Byron White	Retired	Ruth Bader Ginsburg
1994	Bill Clinton	Harry Blackmun	Retired	Stephen Breyer
2005	George W. Bush	William Rehnquist	Died	John Roberts
2006	George W. Bush	Sandra Day O'Connor	Retired	Samuel Alito
2009	Barack Obama	David Souter	Retired	Sonia Sotomayor
2010	Barack Obama	John Paul Stevens	Retired	Elena Kagan

in giving the president the power to nominate and the Senate the power to give 'advice and consent' — and what does that phrase mean anyway? As Charles Gardner Geyh asks in his recent book, *When Courts and Congress Collide* (University of Michigan Press, 2006):

> The appointment process has become a battleground in the struggle for the future of the Court, pitting Democrats against Republicans, the president against the Senate, and the political branches against the judiciary. Given the pervasiveness of customary independence in other contexts, what explains its absence from the appointments process?

But first, let's go back to the origins of the whole thing and try to tease out the intentions of the Founding Fathers.

What the Founding Fathers intended

Article II, Section 2 of the Constitution states that:

> [The President] shall have Power, by and with the Advice and Consent of the Senate, to nominate . . . Judges of the supreme court.

This is not a lot to go on, and contains that somewhat ambiguous phrase 'advice and consent'. This phrase did not spring, newborn, into the Constitution.

Rather it was 'the battle-scarred victor' (Geyh) of many different proposals that competing delegates at the Philadelphia Convention had proposed. At the time of the Convention — 1787 — none of the states had any experience of selecting judges by popular election. As we shall see in Chapter 6, today over 30 states have elections for state judges. But in 1787, the range of options was limited to differing forms of appointment. Three different schemes were given serious consideration by the delegates.

The so-called Virginia Plan called for court appointments to be made by Congress as a whole. This idea was quickly rejected because in the words of convention delegate James Wilson:

> Experience [has] showed the impropriety of such [appointments]. Intrigue, partiality and concealment were the necessary consequences.

A variation on this proposal was then made that only the Senate should have this power, the Senate at the time being an indirectly elected body, thought to be more august and deliberative: in the words of another delegate, Luther Martin, 'best informed of characters and most capable of making a fit choice'. But this proposal, too, was dropped.

The counter-proposal to appointment by the legislature, or part of it, was appointment by the president. This was contained in the so-called New Jersey Plan. The advantage here, argued the supporters, was that judges 'might be appointed by a single, responsible person'. But critics were worried that a court appointed by one person would too much reflect the state from which he came, while others pointed out that 'the Executive will possess neither the requisite knowledge of characters nor confidence of the people for so high a trust'. So this plan, too, was defeated.

Now remember that, in the words of that veteran commentator on all things American, the late Alistair Cooke, the US Constitution is based on three fundamental principles: 'compromise, compromise and compromise'. There were two compromises proposed to these earlier proposals: that the Senate would nominate judges, subject to a veto by the president and a Senate override power; and that the president would nominate judges, subject to Senate approval. And what became the sentence quoted above in Article II, Section 2, was a compromise between the two compromises! Hence the ambiguity: the phrase was a fudge. Both the president and the Senate would play a role in judicial appointments, but it was still not entirely clear what those roles would be.

Here is what Professor Geyh makes of it:

> This was a confederation of odd bedfellows, some of whom had been prepared to entrust the president but not the Senate with the appointment power while

others were prepared to do the opposite. It is thus reasonable to suspect that the original understanding of the Senate's role in rendering 'advice and consent' would vary depending on whether the delegate one asked envisioned a process that minimised Senate interference with presidential prerogatives or one that maximised the Senate's capacity to check presidential power.

So it is hardly surprising that the process has evolved with some degree of uncertainty.

An evolving process

At the Philadelphia Convention, Alexander Hamilton made a prediction that the Senate would play a 'largely silent' role in judicial appointments. At least initially he was correct. For the first 160 years or so — from the presidency of George Washington through Harry Truman — the Senate often did little more than take a vote on the president's nominee, and more often than not this was merely a voice vote, not a recorded vote. In the years from 1789 to 1953, 63 of the 100 votes on Supreme Court justices were voice votes. Of the remaining 37, nine (9%) were rejected. During this period, the Senate's confirmation process was confined pretty much to an evaluation of the nominee's qualifications, character or merit. Only if the nominee was found wanting in one or more of these areas did the Senate play any significant role at all. So, for example, of Franklin Roosevelt's eight Supreme Court nominees between 1937 and 1943 — a surprisingly high number for a 6-year period — only two came to a recorded vote and both were confirmed by overwhelming majorities, one attracting only 16 no votes, the other a mere 4.

But of the 32 Supreme Court nominations that have come to a vote since 1953, only 6 have been approved by a voice vote, and the last of those 6 was Justice Abe Fortas in 1965. All of the 20 most recent Supreme Court nominations that have come to a vote in the Senate chamber have come to a recorded vote and 3 (15%) of those 20 were rejected. Whereas in the first century-and-a-half or so of Court nominations the focus was on qualifications, character and merit, the nature of partisanship in the Senate has meant an increasing focus in the last four decades on the political ideology of the nominees.

Even when the Senate moved in the late 1960s from voice votes to recorded votes, many nominees were still approved almost unanimously. Indeed two of the current members of the Supreme Court attracted not a single 'no vote' between them — Antonin Scalia (98–0) and Anthony Kennedy (97–0). Even as recently as the 1990s, President Clinton's two nominees, Ruth Bader Ginsburg and Stephen Breyer, attracted votes of 96–3 and 87–9 respectively.

| Table 1.2 | Senate confirmation votes on Supreme Court nominees: 1975–2010 | |

Supreme Court nominee	Date	Senate confirmation vote
John Paul Stevens	17 December 1975	98–0
Sandra Day O'Connor	21 September 1981	99–0
William Rehnquist	17 September 1986	65–33
Antonin Scalia	17 September 1986	98–0
Robert Bork	23 October 1987	42–58
Anthony Kennedy	3 February 1988	97–0
David Souter	2 October 1990	90–9
Clarence Thomas	15 October 1991	52–48
Ruth Bader Ginsburg	3 August 1993	96–3
Stephen Breyer	29 July 1994	87–9
John Roberts	29 September 2005	78–22
Samuel Alito	31 January 2006	58–42
Sonia Sotomayor	6 August 2009	68–31
Elena Kagan	5 August 2010	63–37

But the nominations of John Roberts in 2005, Samuel Alito in 2006 and Sonia Sotomayor in 2009 attracted no fewer than 95 'no votes' between them — 22 for Roberts, 31 for Sotomayor and 42 for Alito. The Senate confirmation process had evolved into a partisan battle. How, when and why did this occur?

Bloomberg via Getty Images

The justices of the Supreme Court on 29 September 2009. Seated from left: Kennedy, Stevens (retired 2010), Roberts, Scalia and Thomas. Standing: Alito, Ginsburg, Breyer and Sotomayor.

The Bork nomination

The watershed in the nomination and confirmation process of Supreme Court justices came in 1987 with President Reagan's nomination to the Supreme Court of Robert Bork. It was a watershed for a number of reasons.

First, it was a watershed in the way presidents would stress the ideology of their Supreme Court nominees. President Reagan introduced Bork at a White House ceremony on 1 July 1987 by stating that Bork was 'widely regarded as the most prominent and intellectually powerful advocate of judicial restraint in the country'. That put ideology fairly and squarely at the centre of the Bork nomination.

Second, it was a watershed in the way interest groups would get involved in the pro- and anti-campaigns to support or oppose Supreme Court nominees. Gregory Peck, who was a far more famous Hollywood actor than Ronald Reagan had ever been, became the face and the voice of a $200,000 anti-Bork TV commercial campaign which claimed amongst other things about Robert Bork:

> He defended poll taxes and literacy tests which kept many [African-] Americans from voting. He opposed the civil rights law that ended 'White Only' signs at lunch counters.

The American Conservative Union shot back with ads declaring:

> He is probably the greatest legal scholar of our time — probably the most qualified nominee within the last 50 years.

Third, it was a watershed in the media coverage of the confirmation hearings. They covered them in a way which looked more like a World Wrestling Entertainment event than a thoughtful debate among the great and the good over judicial merit and qualification. The Cable-Satellite Public Affairs Network (commonly known as C-SPAN) had started live, gavel-to-gavel coverage of the Senate just 15 months before the Bork hearings opened on Capitol Hill. When Bork was introduced at the Senate Judiciary Committee hearings on 15 September 1987 by former President Ford, there were more than two dozen television cameras pointed at Bork. That evening on *NBC News*, anchor Tom Brokaw claimed in rather exaggerated prose:

> The nomination of Robert Bork is a struggle for the philosophical soul of the US Supreme Court. It is a test of Ronald Reagan's political power in the closing days of his administration.

Finally, it was a watershed in the way in which Senate confirmation hearings of Supreme Court nominees would be characterised by partisanship and a lack of civility — and, some might say, honesty. This was nowhere more clearly seen than in a speech made by the late Senator Edward Kennedy on the floor of the Senate:

> Robert Bork's America is a land in which women would be forced into back-alley abortions, blacks would sit at segregated lunch counters, rogue police could break down citizens' doors in midnight raids, school children could not be taught evolution, writers and artists could be censored at the whim of the government and the doors of the federal courts would be shut on the fingers of millions of citizens for whom the judiciary is — and is often the only — protector of the individual rights that are at the heart of our democracy.

Fortunately, Bork resisted the temptation to respond with his own view of what 'Ted Kennedy's America' might look like! But despite Bork's confidence that he would be confirmed, his nomination was defeated on the Senate floor by 42 votes to 58, the biggest vote against a Supreme Court nominee in history.

Bork had been proved wrong in his confidence that he would be confirmed, but he was pretty quickly proved right about one thing. Following his defeat, Bork made the prediction that 'the tendency [in future] will be to nominate and confirm persons whose performance once on the bench cannot be accurately, or perhaps even roughly, predicted by the president or by the Senate'. And so it was with the next Court nominee, President George H. W. Bush's nomination in 1990 of David Souter: an obscure New Hampshire judge, about whom so little was known that he was widely described as Bush's 'stealth candidate', a sort of closet conservative. He proved to be a reliable *liberal* vote for most of his 19 years on the Court. And then there was Clarence Thomas.

'A high-tech lynching'

In 1991, Thurgood Marshall — the first African-American to serve on the Supreme Court — resigned. Marshall had served 24 years since his appointment by President Johnson in 1967 and had become a strong and much-respected voice defending the rights and liberties of minorities and the disadvantaged in American society. He was a reliable vote with the liberal wing of the Court.

To replace Justice Marshall, President George H. W. Bush nominated Clarence Thomas, another African-American — a federal circuit judge and former head of the Equal Employment Opportunity Commission. But Thomas was as much to the right in his ideology as Marshall had been to the left. Democrats — and especially liberal Democrats and African-Americans — were infuriated. Thomas's confirmation hearings were an explosive event, with Democrats accusing him of sexual harassment towards a former work colleague, Anita Hill. But in Thomas's view, it was all about ideology and he ended by describing the confirmation process in the following colourful language:

> This is not an opportunity to talk about difficult matters privately or in a closed environment. This is a circus. It's a national disgrace. And from my standpoint, as a black American, it is a high-tech lynching for uppity blacks who in any way deign to think for themselves, to do for themselves, to have different ideas, and it is a message that unless you kowtow to an old order, this is what will happen to you. You will be lynched, destroyed, caricatured by a committee of the US Senate rather than hung from a tree.

Thomas was confirmed — just — by a 52–48 vote in the Senate chamber. But the Bork and Thomas hearings left a legacy that would colour the nomination and confirmation process for decades to come. This is how Charles G. Geyh summed it up in his 2006 book:

> The Bork and Thomas confirmation fights led by Senate Democrats and leftward leaning interest groups left Senate Republicans deeply resentful, and it was widely anticipated that 'payback' would be forthcoming.

But when two vacancies occurred in the first 2 years of Bill Clinton's presidency, the president avoided any damaging fights with Senate Republicans by consulting widely with Senate leaders from both sides of the aisle and nominating on each occasion a well-qualified and consensus candidate — Ruth Bader Ginsburg (1993) and Stephen Breyer (1994) — who evoked little of significant controversy or opposition.

George W. Bush took a similar line in nominating John Roberts to the Court in 2005, but his nomination of Samuel Alito in 2006 and Barack Obama's nomination of Sonia Sotomayor in 2009 saw reoccurrences of the partisan bickering over judicial nominees that seems to have become part of the process.

What is wrong with the process?

It is possible to identify three specific things that are wrong with the nomination and confirmation process for members of the Supreme Court, and these weaknesses and problems affect all the various players in the process — the president, the Senate, interest groups and the media.

Presidents tend to politicise the nomination process

Modern-day presidents have mostly tried to pick Court nominees who fit their own political and judicial philosophy. Indeed, they have often made a virtue of this, even promising to do so during their election campaigns. Here's Democratic presidential candidate Al Gore campaigning in Michigan during the 2000 election:

> The Supreme Court is at stake [in this election]. There are going to be three, maybe four justices of the Supreme Court appointed by the next president of the United States. That means a majority on the Court that will interpret our rights under our Constitution for the next 30 to 40 years.

Meanwhile, the Republican candidate in the same election, Governor George W. Bush, was making clear to voters how he would pick Supreme Court nominees. During a campaign speech, Mr Bush stated: 'I'm going to name strict constructionists.' Speaking with reporters after the speech, Bush defined a strict constructionist as a judge who 'doesn't use the opportunity of the Constitution to pass legislation or legislate from the bench.' He continued:

> That's going to be a big difference between my opponent and me. I don't believe in liberal, activist judges.

When Bush was asked which Supreme Court justices he most admired, he named conservatives Antonin Scalia and Clarence Thomas.

Eight years later, candidate Barack Obama named his favourite justices during his presidential election campaign. Speaking at a campaign stop in Michigan in October 2008, Barack Obama had this to say:

> When I think about the kinds of judges who are needed today, it goes back to the point I was making about common sense and pragmatism as opposed to ideology. I think that Justice Souter, who was a Republican appointee, Justice Breyer, a Democratic appointee, are very sensible judges. They take a look at the facts and they try to figure out: How does the Constitution apply to these facts? They believe in fidelity to the text of the Constitution, but they also think you have to look at what is going on around you and not just ignore real life. That, I think, is the kind of justice that I'm looking for — somebody who respects the law, doesn't think that they should be making law, but also has a sense of what's happening in the real world and recognises that one of the roles of the courts is to protect people who don't have a voice.

So it is hardly surprising that, once elected to office and faced with filling a vacancy on the Supreme Court, presidents try to keep their promises and political ideology becomes an important — maybe *the most* important — ingredient in their selection process. Indeed, it is feared that sometimes, as in the case of the nominations of Clarence Thomas by the first President Bush in 1990 and of Harriet Miers by the second President Bush in 2005, ideology trumps qualification and merit.

True, there have been examples in recent times when presidents have chosen highly qualified nominees who have not raised allegations of overt partisanship. President Clinton's nominations of Ruth Bader Ginsburg (1993) and Stephen Breyer (1994) as well as George W. Bush's nomination of John Roberts (2005) come to mind. But for every Ginsburg, Breyer or Roberts, there is a Bork, Thomas or Alito — and probably a Sotomayor.

The Senate tends to politicise the confirmation process

You do not have to agree with Justice Clarence Thomas's rasping critique of the Senate confirmation process, quoted above, to agree with this second claim that the Senate tends to politicise the confirmation process. And this has been especially noticeable since the late 1980s — since the Bork confirmation hearings. The Senate Judiciary Committee hearings, the debate on the Senate floor and the resulting votes have all come to be marked by high levels of partisanship. Put simply, members of the president's party spend much of their time in verbose congratulation of the nominee and throwing soft-ball questions at them, while the opposition party ask what they hope will be 'gotcha' questions — more interested in embarrassing or catching out the nominee than in participating in careful oversight and scrutiny of the nominee's merit and qualifications.

We can illustrate some of these problems from the hearings held to confirm Samuel Alito to the Supreme Court in 2006. Here is an exchange between Judge Alito and Republican senator Charles Grassley of Iowa during the second day of the committee hearings:

> GRASSLEY: Judge Alito, do you believe that the executive branch should have unchecked authority?
>
> ALITO: Absolutely not, Senator.
>
> GRASSLEY: Judge Alito, do you understand that when constitutionally protected rights are involved, the courts have an important role to play in making sure that the executive branch does not trample those rights?

ALITO: I certainly do, Senator.

GRASSLEY: Do you believe that the president of the United States is above the law and the Constitution?

ALITO: Nobody in this country is above the law, and that includes the president.

So Judge Alito believes in checks and balances, civil rights and equality before the law. Whatever next? What we have here is a senator from the president's party asking sit-up-and-beg questions which, quite frankly, a sixth-grade civics student could answer.

Meanwhile, the Democrats were busy trying to catch out Judge Alito — to make him out as some kind of bigot, maybe a racist, or even a misogynist. 'Are you perhaps a closet bigot?' asked Republican senator Lindsey Graham of South Carolina, trying to embarrass his Democrat colleagues for asking what he doubtless regarded as tactless and embarrassing questions. And when it was all over, an editorial in the *Washington Post* summed it up thus:

> The hearings were less illuminating than might have been hoped. Democratic senators often seemed more interested in attacking the nominee — sometimes scurrilously — than in probing what sort of justice he would be. Republican senators, meanwhile, acted more as fatuous counsels for the defence than as sober evaluators of a nominee to serve on the Supreme Court. On both sides, pious, meandering speeches outnumbered thoughtful questions. As a result, Americans don't know all that much more about Judge Alito than they did before.

Justice Sonia Sotomayor

And when all was said and done, the Senate confirmed Judge Alito on what was virtually a party-line vote with all bar one Republican voting 'yes' and all bar four Democrats voting 'no'.

A few years ago, Calvin Mackenzie published a book with the title, *Innocent Until Nominated: The Breakdown of the Presidential Appointment Process* (Brookings Institution Press, 2001). His conclusion was that the confirmation process was character-ised by 'invasive scrutiny' and 'cruel and punishing publicity' for the nominee, which discourages some people from even being prepared to be nominated for high office and thereby 'hinders the president's ability to govern.'

There is too much influence from interest groups and the media

The day after President Barack Obama nominated Sonia Sotomayor to the Supreme Court, the *Washington Post* had an article with the headline: 'Battle Lines Are Drawn On Sotomayor Nomination'. Within 24 hours of the nomination being announced from the White House, the first television advertisements appeared in support of Judge Sotomayor courtesy of the Coalition for Constitutional Values.

The trouble with most interest group involvement in the Supreme Court confirmation process is that it tends to represent only the interests of those at both ends of the extreme in the arguments. Take a sampling of interest group statements on the nomination of Judge Sonia Sotomayor in 2009. Nan Aron, president of the liberal group, the Alliance for Justice, stated:

> President Obama has nominated a highly qualified candidate with a compelling personal story and outstanding educational credentials. Judge Sotomayor has more federal judicial experience than any justice nominated to the Supreme Court in the past 100 years. The nomination shows that President Obama is appointing judges who understand that the role of the courts is to give everyone a chance to be heard, to stand up for their rights, and get justice.

You would hardly recognise the same story if you listened to what Wendy Long, counsel to the right-wing Judicial Confirmation Network, had to say:

> Judge Sotomayor is a liberal judicial activist of the first order who thinks her own personal political agenda is more important than the law as written. She thinks that judges should dictate policy, and that one's sex, race and ethnicity ought to affect the decisions one renders from the bench. She reads racial preferences and quotas into the Constitution.

The 24/7 news media, including such organisations and media outlets as CNN, Fox News, talk radio, bloggers and twitters, promote their own angle on the nominee, pandering to whichever view they tend to reflect (see Box 1.1). Right-wing radio talk show host Rush Limbaugh, for example, compared Sonia Sotomayor to former Ku Klux Klan leader David Duke, suggesting she was what he called 'a reverse racist', while former Republican House Speaker Newt Gingrich took a similar line on Twitter calling Judge Sotomayor 'a Latina woman racist' — not exactly helpful to promoting balanced and thoughtful debate of the nominee's qualifications and merit for the highest court in the nation.

Box 1.1

Text of story from American Public Media regarding interest group and media involvement in the Sotomayor nomination, 2009

Interest groups battle over Sotomayor

KAI RYSSDAL: With the President's announcement yesterday that Federal Appeals Court Judge Sonia Sotomayor is in line for a promotion, the money machine is kicking into gear. Over the past couple of decades, Supreme Court nominations have featured big media buys and non-stop cable chatter. Marketplace's Steve Henn reports one reason for that — some big institutions have a vested interest in cheering on the fight.

STEVE HENN: The first TV ads in support of Judge Sonia Sotomayor's nomination to the Supreme Court hit the air today, less than 24 hours after word of her nomination leaked out. The ad's text highlights Sotomayor's accomplishments, like serving as a prosecutor and graduating from Princeton and Yale. It was paid for by the liberal group, the Coalition for Constitutional Values. In the past two decades, roughly a dozen different non-profit organisations across the political spectrum have set up in Washington with the goal of pushing their judicial agenda. Call it the Supreme Court Nomination Industrial Complex. These groups exist to influence nomination fights. But they also depend on these fights to raise money and survive.

RICHARD VIGUERIE: Opportunities like this seldom come along.

HENN: Conservative activist Richard Viguerie runs a direct mail firm. He's using it to fan the flames of opposition and raise cash. And when it comes to encouraging controversy over Court nominations, political partisans have plenty of company. John Morton is a columnist at the *American Journalism Review*.

JOHN MORTON: The media like conflict, wherever it comes from and regardless of how phony it might be.

HENN: Commercials about the last couple of Supreme Court nominations — John Roberts and Samuel Alito — have cost about a million dollars each but insiders say those ads brought in even more cash.

Source: **http://marketplace.publicradio.org**, Wednesday, 27 May 2009

It was the same conservative interest groups and talk show hosts who lambasted President George W. Bush for his choice of Harriet Miers to fill the vacancy created by the retirement of Justice Sandra Day O'Connor in 2005. Their opposition had such a galvanising effect among Senate Republicans that President Bush was pressured into withdrawing the nomination. Speaking on NBC's *Meet the Press* on 9 October 2005, conservative commentator Pat Buchanan complained:

> You've got [people like] Priscilla Owen, Janice Rogers Brown, Samuel Alito, countless others we've been preparing who are as certain in their judicial philosophy as Robert Bork was, and then we get handed a blank slate whose commendation, according to White House briefers, is that she's never taken a stand. This White House has ducked the fight. The President has recoiled from greatness. He has retreated into the old politics of compromise and consensus on what for us was the greatest issue of his second term.

Here we have a president being criticised for not being sufficiently partisan by those from within the base of his own party. Partisan supporters do not want statesmanship and bipartisanship; they prefer red meat.

Why then do interest groups participate in the judicial nomination and confirmation process? This is how Professor Karen O'Connor answers that question in her contribution to the 2005 edition of *The Interest Group Connection* (CQ Press):

> Most groups that participate in the process intend that like-minded men and women reach the Supreme Court, because any one of them may play a central role in shaping policies of great importance to a group. In addition to attempting to manipulate the press, media, and therefore public opinion during the judicial nominating process, organised groups also participate extensively in the formal confirmation process.

There were, for example, 76 interest groups that appeared in the Senate Judiciary Committee hearings on the nomination of Clarence Thomas in 1991, but even that was fewer than the 86 that appeared at the Bork hearings in 1986. In contrast, John Paul Stevens' confirmation hearings back in 1975 attracted input from just five interest groups.

Conclusion

Nominations to the Supreme Court are almost bound to create a good deal of fervent interest. They are lifetime appointments to a nine-member body that has the power to declare Acts of Congress unconstitutional and, in effect, to amend the Constitution through interpretation. One is reminded of Charles Evans Hughes's famous remark that Americans are 'under a Constitution, but the Constitution is what the judges say it is'. That being so, nominations are inevitably of great importance.

But how to improve the process? First, presidents would be well advised to nominate only those jurists who are unquestionably of the highest qualification and merit, with no political, personal or judicial baggage. President George

W. Bush's nomination of John Roberts in 2005 managed to attract the votes of half the Senate Democrats simply because he was such a stellar candidate. Presidents get themselves into difficulty when they nominate the overtly controversial (Robert Bork), the professionally lightweight (Clarence Thomas) or the virtually anonymous crony (Harriet Miers).

Second, the Senate needs to look to reform its confirmation process. The judiciary committee hearings are based on a dull and turgid formula, featuring far too much posing by senators. The membership of the committee is overtly partisan, and the members too often loquacious. The hearings need to focus on qualification and merit, not on scandal and gossip.

Third, what can be done about interest groups and the media? There one probably draws something of a blank. Segregation may have largely disappeared from American society, but it is alive and well in the halls of the media and interest groups, which pander to the tastes of their ideologically homogeneous admirers. On 17 July 2009, the highly respected anchorman of the *CBS Evening News*, Walter Cronkite, died at the age of 92. The era of Uncle Walter is over. The era of Rush Limbaugh and Glenn Beck is truly upon us, and with it a somewhat gloomy prospect for the future of national discourse on nominations to the US Supreme Court.

Task 1.1

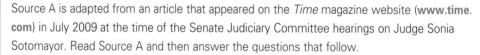

Source A is adapted from an article that appeared on the *Time* magazine website (**www.time.com**) in July 2009 at the time of the Senate Judiciary Committee hearings on Judge Sonia Sotomayor. Read Source A and then answer the questions that follow.

Source A
Sotomayor keeps her cool on the Senate hot seat

Whatever Sonia Sotomayor does to reward herself — a glass of wine, an ice cream sundae, a bubble bath — surely she must be giving herself a small pat on the back after surviving her first day of cross-examination by the Senate Judiciary Committee without any kind of gaffe. Despite the best efforts of Republicans to elicit a hot-tempered response, the Supreme Court nominee answered every question in the same deliberate, dulcet tones that seemed to lull her opposition into, if not complacency, then at least resignation.

The Democratic senators spent much of the day alternatively praising Sotomayor and attacking the Roberts-led court. New York Democratic senator Charles Schumer spent the bulk of his time working to dispel the Republican notion of Sotomayor as ruled by passion more than the law. He went through some of Sotomayor's most tragic cases to underline instances where she applied the rule of law even when the decision went against those who had clearly suffered. 'You heard the case of families of the 213 victims of the tragic TWA crash,' Schumer said. 'The relatives of the victims sued the manufacturers of the airplane, which spontaneously combusted in midair, in order to get some modicum of

Task 1.1 (continued)

relief, though, of course, nothing a court could do would make up for the loss of the loved ones. Did you have sympathy for those families?'

'All of America did,' Sotomayor replied.

'But ultimately, you ruled against them, didn't you?' Schumer asked, knowing her answer would be yes.

(a) What does Source A show about the way senators from the president's party tend to ask questions of Supreme Court nominees?

(b) How is the same point illustrated by the exchange between Republican senator Charles Grassley and Judge Samuel Alito in 2006, quoted earlier in the chapter?

Guidance

In this exercise, you need to keep in mind who the president was who had nominated each particular justice, which party the president belonged to and the party of the particular senator engaging in the questioning of the nominee.

Task 1.2

- Go to the Senate website at **www.senate.gov**.
- Click on 'Committees'.
- Click on 'Judiciary'.
- Click on 'Nominations' and then on 'Supreme Court'.
- Click on 'Committee votes on Recent Supreme Court Nominations'.

From the data provided here, analyse the extent to which the Senate Judiciary Committee has in recent times taken a partisan view of Supreme Court nominees.

Guidance

Once again, you need to think 'party' — the party of the incumbent president and the party of the Judiciary Committee members. Look particularly at the votes cast by the senators from the 'opposition party', i.e. the party not controlling the White House at the time. You could work out for each vote what percentage of the opposition party's senators supported and opposed the nominee. Likewise, see what level of support the senators from the president's party gave to each nominee.

Task 1.3

Source B is adapted from George C. Edwards, *Governing by Campaigning: The Politics of the Bush Presidency* (Pearson Longman, 2007). Read Source B and then answer the questions that follow.

Task 1.3 (continued)

Source B

One bright spot for the White House was the confirmation of John Roberts as chief justice. Democrats and their supporting coalition of interest groups faced a dilemma regarding Roberts. Although they would have preferred a less conservative nominee, Bush was certainly going to name a conservative under any circumstances. In addition, Roberts did not appear to be a fire-breathing radical. Moreover, the nomination came at a time when some Democrats were seeking to soft-pedal their rhetoric on abortion and appeal to more conservative voters. These Democrats did not want to fight a highly visible battle over the issue of abortion, religion and related issues. On the other hand, traditional liberal advocacy groups and many grass-roots activists wanted to fight, and at one point they badly overreached. NARAL Pro-Choice America launched a television ad that accused Roberts of siding with violent extremists and a convicted abortion clinic bomber while serving in the solicitor general's office in Washington DC, an accusation that Roberts' supporters immediately condemned as a flagrant distortion. Soon thereafter, NARAL pulled the ad off the air. In the end, all the Senate Republicans and half the Democrats supported Roberts.

(a) What does this extract tell us about the way both Democrats and Republicans consider the ideology of a Supreme Court nominee during the confirmation process?

(b) Why do you think 'some Democrats were seeking to soft-pedal their rhetoric on abortion and appeal to more conservative voters' at this particular time?

(c) What does the extract tell us about what was wrong with the way the Roberts nomination was handled by this particular liberal interest group?

Guidance

(a) You need to remember that President Bush was a Republican.

(b) Think about the chronology. The Roberts nomination was made in September 2005. Think what was coming up electorally the following year. Then, beyond that, what might have further affected Democrats' thinking in trying to win over independent and conservative voters?

(c) Think how most Americans, certainly independent and conservative voters, would react to this type of allegation.

2 Can a president influence the political balance of the Supreme Court?

> The stakes here are immense — whether or not this President can leave behind a Supreme Court that will carry forward the ideas of the Reagan Revolution into the 21st century.

So wrote Pat Buchanan, then the White House communications director in the Reagan administration, in a 1985 memo to White House Chief of Staff Don Regan. He continued:

> Given the importance of the Supreme Court to the Right-to-Life movement, the School Prayer movement etc. — all of whom provide the Republicans with decisive margins [in elections] — the significance of this nomination is not easy to exaggerate.

He was writing at the moment when Chief Justice Warren Burger had just announced his retirement and President Reagan therefore had the opportunity to nominate a new member of the Court as well as naming the new chief justice. Clearly, Pat Buchanan believed that a president *can* influence the political balance of the Supreme Court. But was he correct?

This is a much-asked question and one to which an overly simplistic answer is often given. The overly simplistic answer goes something like this: the president has the power of appointment to the Supreme Court; the Senate rarely rejects his nominees; presidents choose judges who share their judicial and political philosophy; therefore presidents can change the political balance of the Court. Well, things are not quite that simple and some of those assertions are at best misleading, and at worst just wrong. A more accurate and detailed answer would suggest that for a president to change the political balance of the Supreme Court to his liking, at least four requirements have to be fulfilled. We shall examine each in turn.

Requirements for a president to change the political balance of the Supreme Court

A vacancy must occur

This may seem an obvious point, but it is one worth making. Because Supreme Court justices — like all federal judges — enjoy life tenure on the Court, they cannot be removed from the Court against their will, except by impeachment by the House of Representatives and being found guilty by a two-thirds majority of the Senate. Judges cannot be forced to retire, even when they reach a great age. On 20 April 2010, Justice John Paul Stevens celebrated his ninetieth birthday, but was still serving on the Supreme Court — as he had done for the past 35 years. Justices can retire voluntarily — as Sandra Day O'Connor did in 2005 and as David Souter did in 2009. Justices may die in office — as 80-year-old Chief Justice William Rehnquist did in September 2005.

William Rehnquist, Chief Justice, 1986–2005

When Sandra O'Connor announced her retirement in July 2005, this created the first vacancy on the Court for 11 years. Now admittedly, this was an unusually long period of time to go without a vacancy occurring, but it meant that President Clinton appointed no Supreme Court justices during his second term and President George W. Bush appointed none during his first term.

After John Paul Stevens was appointed to the Supreme Court in 1975 by President Ford, the next vacancy did not occur on the Court until 1981 — the first year of Reagan's presidency. But that 6-year gap meant that one-term president Jimmy Carter (1977–81) made no appointments at all to the Supreme Court. So there was no way Jimmy Carter could change the balance of the Supreme Court. And clearly, the more vacancies that occur during a presidency, the greater chance a president will have of changing the Court's balance, other things being equal. President Nixon's just over 5½ years in office — January 1969 to August 1974 — saw four vacancies come up, as did President Reagan's 8 years (see Table 2.1). Nixon and Reagan, therefore, had a better chance of reshaping the Court than did Clinton and George W. Bush, who appointed only four justices between them in 16 years.

Of course, presidents might wish that a justice would retire. George W. Bush must surely have wished that liberal justice John Paul Stevens — already 80 when Bush arrived at the White House in 2001 — would have retired during

Table 2.1 Number of Supreme Court vacancies per presidency: 1961–2010

President	Dates	Party	Supreme Court vacancies
John Kennedy	1961–63	Dem	2
Lyndon Johnson	1963–69	Dem	2
Richard Nixon	1969–74	R	4
Gerald Ford	1974–77	R	1
Jimmy Carter	1977–81	Dem	0
Ronald Reagan	1981–89	R	4
George H. W. Bush	1989–93	R	2
Bill Clinton	1993–2001	Dem	2
George W. Bush	2001–09	R	2
Barack Obama	2009–	Dem	2*

*to 31 May 2010

his presidency. But Stevens was still going strong at 88 when Bush bowed out at the end of his two terms.

Franklin Roosevelt had a different idea. Just after his landslide re-election in 1936, and facing opposition from the older members of the Court to his New Deal, Roosevelt proposed the Judiciary Reorganisation Bill to Congress. There had been no vacancies on the Supreme Court during Roosevelt's first term. The bill aimed to overhaul and modernise the federal judiciary, but hidden within it was a provision allowing the president to appoint a new justice for each one who did not retire within 6 months of reaching 70 years of age, up to a maximum of six. Congress saw it for what it was, and the bill was defeated. It will always be remembered by the soubriquet of 'the court-packing plan'. No president has ever attempted to pull such a stunt since then. Presidents must wait for a vacancy, and this in itself is a barrier to the president's ability to influence the political balance of the Court.

The new appointee must have a different judicial philosophy from their predecessor

This is a most important point and is almost always overlooked in discussions on Supreme Court appointments. First, we need to clarify what we mean by 'judicial philosophy'. Simply put, we can think of justices of the Supreme Court as being strict constructionists or loose constructionists depending on how they view the way one is supposed to interpret the Constitution in deciding cases. Strict constructions — often described as conservatives — interpret the Constitution in a strict or literal sense. They place much emphasis on what the original text says — hence they are sometimes described as 'originalists'. Loose constructionists, on the other hand — often described as liberals — interpret the Constitution in a loose, less literal sense. They see it as their role to read things into the original text because society has moved on and the Constitution needs to be read in its modern context. A simple way of understanding the difference between the two is that strict constructionists emphasise the *text* whereas loose constructionists emphasise the *context*. Republican presidents tend to appoint the former; Democrat presidents the latter. We shall have more to say on this matter in Chapter 3.

So in the context of the question posed at the start of this chapter, Republican presidents want to make the Court more conservative, made up of more strict constructionists; Democrat presidents want to make the Court more liberal, made up of more loose constructionists. Now if the president is to change the political and judicial philosophy of the Court, then the new appointee must have a different philosophy from their predecessor. Let's illustrate this point with some recent examples.

President George W. Bush made two appointments to the Supreme Court during his presidency. First, he appointed John Roberts to replace Chief Justice William Rehnquist. Rehnquist was a Nixon appointee and had been on the Court for 34 years, serving as chief justice for the last 19 of those years. Rehnquist was a strict constructionist — a conservative justice. It was clear that his replacement, John Roberts, was of the same judicial and political philosophy. The way he would decide cases would not be distinctly different from the way Rehnquist had decided them. Therefore by replacing one conservative with another, President Bush was not really able to change the ideological balance of the Court.

Bush's second appointment was of Samuel Alito to replace Associate Justice Sandra Day O'Connor. O'Connor was a Reagan appointee and had been on the Court for 24 years. But O'Connor was not a typical conservative justice. She not infrequently voted with her more liberal colleagues, especially when it came to cases dealing with abortion and affirmative action. But Alito has proven — at least in his first four terms on the Court — to be a reliably conservative justice. And in the years since Alito has joined the Supreme Court, there is quite a bit of evidence that Bush's appointment of Alito for O'Connor has changed the political balance of the Court.

In the Court's 2005–06 term, in the case of *Hudson* v *Michigan*, the Court ruled — by 5 votes to 4 — that the Constitution does not require evidence gained through what are called 'no knock' searches to be excluded from the courtroom. This was something of a reversal of what is called the 'exclusionary rule', for in previous cases the Court had interpreted the Fourth Amendment as protecting citizens from 'no knock' searches. A number of commentators at the time of this decision suggested that Justice O'Connor would have disagreed with the majority decision in this case and joined the dissenting liberals — David Souter, John Paul Stevens, Ruth Bader Ginsburg and Stephen Breyer — thus making theirs the majority opinion.

There was even more evidence of the shift in balance in the Court as a result of the Alito for O'Connor switch in the Court's 2006–07 term. In the case of *Gonzales* v *Carhart*, the Court upheld the Partial-Birth Abortion Ban Act — a federal law banning this particular late-term abortion procedure. The 5–4 majority decision was authored by Justice Anthony Kennedy, and he was joined by the Court's conservative quartet of John Roberts, Antonin Scalia, Clarence Thomas and Samuel Alito. But back in 2000, when Justice O'Connor was still on the Court, the Court had struck down a Nebraska state law prohibiting the same late-term abortion procedure. The 2000 decision of *Stenberg* v *Carhart* was also a 5–4 decision, but on that occasion the liberal wing of the Court — justices Souter, Stevens, Ginsburg and Breyer — joined by Justice O'Connor were in the majority. Joan Biskupic, in her editorial comment in *USA Today* after the *Gonzales* decision in 2007, wrote:

> The Supreme Court's abortion ruling was a reminder of the Court's rightward turn since the addition of Bush's appointee Samuel Alito.

Further evidence emerged in 2007–08 in the case of *Davis* v *Federal Election Commission*. In yet another 5–4 decision, the Court declared the so-called 'millionaire's amendment' of the Bipartisan Campaign Reform Act (BCRA) — commonly known as the McCain–Feingold Act — to be unconstitutional. Samuel Alito authored the majority opinion in this case, joined by Anthony Kennedy and his three conservative colleagues. But back in 2003, in *McConnell* v *Federal Election Commission*, Justice O'Connor had authored a 5–4 majority which substantially upheld the provisions of BCRA. On that occasion, O'Connor had again sided with the four liberal justices.

There was even more startling evidence of the significance of the Alito for O'Connor switch in the landmark First Amendment case of *Citizens United* v *Federal Election Commission* (2010) — yet another decision concerning the McCain–Feingold Act. In a 5–4 decision, the Court struck down an important provision of the Act — the one which had barred the airing of issue-orientated television advertisements, paid for by corporations or trade unions, 30 days before a primary and 60 days before a general election. In the 2003 case, Justice O'Connor had joined the Court's four liberals to uphold this ban; now Samuel

Alito joined the Court's four conservatives to strike down the ban. 'The decision is a telling reminder of how quickly the Supreme Court has changed,' wrote Robert Barnes and Dan Eggen in the *Washington Post* ('Supreme Court rejects limits on corporate spending on political campaigns', 22 January 2010) the following day. Justice John Paul Stevens was even more blunt when he stated in his dissent that 'the only relevant thing that has changed [since the previous campaign finance decisions] is the composition of this Court'.

President Obama's nomination of Judge Sonia Sotomayor to replace Justice David Souter on the Supreme Court is unlikely to have been a Court-changing appointment. Just as the Roberts for Rehnquist swap by President Bush in 2005 was one conservative for another, so the Sotomayor for Souter swap by President Obama was one liberal — albeit a moderate one — for another. One could see some evidence for this even before Judge Sotomayor joined the Supreme Court.

In 2009 in *Ricci* v *DeStefano*, the Court reversed a federal appeal court decision in which Judge Sotomayor had earlier concurred. The case concerned the matter of race in the hiring and promotion of workers in the public sector — in this case, firefighters in New Haven, Connecticut; in other words, it was about the constitutional status of affirmative action programmes. But the justice whom Judge Sotomayor would later replace on the Supreme Court, David Souter, disagreed with the majority decision in the *Ricci* case. Put another way, he voted to uphold a decision made by his successor. It would appear, therefore, that justices Souter and Sotomayor are not significantly different in the way they make their decisions. So, for a president to change the balance of the Court, this particular requirement must be present.

Table 2.2 looks at the Supreme Court replacements that occurred between 1975 and 2010, and attempts to judge whether or not the replacement constituted a change in judicial philosophy. Clearly this table needs to have a health warning attached to it. One really cannot pigeonhole every Supreme Court justice for the last four decades in a word — be it liberal, swing, conservative or maverick. In some — though not in all — cases, we are making wild generalisations. But the table nonetheless shows a clear trend.

The trend is that on very few occasions in the last 35 years have presidents been able to effect a change of judicial philosophy on the Court through an appointment they have made. Of the 13 Supreme Court appointments made during this 35-year period, in only two, maybe three, did the appointment signal a philosophical shift. The Alito for O'Connor change we have already discussed. The most startling change was in President George H. W. Bush's appointment of Clarence Thomas to replace Thurgood Marshall in 1991.

Supreme Court replacements: 1975–2010

Year	Justice retired/died	Type	Justice appointed	Type	Change?
2010	John Paul Stevens	Liberal	Elena Kagan	Liberal	No
2009	David Souter	Liberal	Sonia Sotomayor	Liberal	No
2006	Sandra Day O'Connor	Swing	Samuel Alito	Conservative	Yes
2005	William Rehnquist	Conservative	John Roberts	Conservative	No
1994	Harry Blackmun	Cons to Lib	Stephen Breyer	Liberal	No?
1993	Byron White	Maverick	Ruth Bader Ginsburg	Liberal	Yes, a bit
1991	Thurgood Marshall	Liberal	Clarence Thomas	Conservative	Yes
1990	William Brennan	Liberal	David Souter	Liberal	No
1988	Lewis Powell	Moderate	Anthony Kennedy	Moderate	No
1986	William Rehnquist*	Conservative	Antonin Scalia	Conservative	No
1986	Warren Burger	Conservative	William Rehnquist	Conservative	No
1981	Potter Stewart	Swing	Sandra Day O'Connor	Swing	No
1975	William Douglas	Liberal	John Paul Stevens	Liberal	No

*Appointed Chief Justice (remained on the Court)

This constituted replacing the Court's leading liberal with someone who would become one of the Court's arch conservatives. Other than their race — both were African-Americans — Marshall and Thomas had virtually nothing in common. Thomas's elevation to the Supreme Court pushed the Court significantly to the right. Two years later, maybe President Clinton's replacement of Byron White with Ruth Bader Ginsburg tilted the Court slightly to the left. Clinton's other Court appointee, Stephen Breyer, replaced the by-then liberal Harry Blackmun. Blackmun began as a conservative, but ended as a liberal, having authored the famous *Roe* v *Wade* decision in 1973. We shall have more to say of justices who evolve in a later section.

The Senate must confirm the appointment

Nominating justices to the Supreme Court is only half of the process — and the easy half at that. Getting them confirmed by the Senate can be a much bigger challenge, especially if the president faces a Senate controlled by the other party. Four of the last seven presidents (not counting Obama) who have made Supreme Court appointments have encountered difficulties in the Senate. Democrat President Johnson ran into difficulties trying to promote his friend Abe Fortas to the post of Chief Justice. The nomination was filibustered by both Republicans and southern Democrats, and Fortas eventually withdrew following allegations of financial impropriety.

Republican President Nixon managed to lose two Supreme Court nominations within 5 months of each other as the Democrat-controlled Senate defeated two conservative southern judges — Clement Haynsworth and Harrold Carswell. Haynsworth was an ultra-conservative from South Carolina, whilst Carswell suffered from being not only far too conservative but also patently unqualified. It was of Judge Carswell that Senator Hruska of Nebraska said, in trying to offer some support to the nominee, that even if Carswell were mediocre, mediocre people 'are entitled to a little representation' on the Court. Haynsworth was defeated 45–55 and Carswell went down by 45 votes to 51.

President Reagan lost two Supreme Court nominees as well — these within 2 weeks of each other. The Republican president, who had enjoyed his own party being in the majority in the Senate for the first 6 years of his presidency, now — in 1987 — found the Democrats in the driving seat. He lost his nomination of Robert Bork to the Supreme Court in a 42–58 vote on 23 October, only to see his next nominee Douglas Ginsburg have to withdraw in early November after allegations of illegal drug use.

And in 2005, President George W. Bush suffered the indignity of seeing one of his Court nominees, Harriet Miers, withdraw after fierce opposition from members of his own — Republican — party. So even having party control of the Senate is no guarantee of safe passage for Supreme Court nominees. Given the judicial importance and life tenure of Supreme Court justices, the Senate takes its 'advice and consent' power over them more seriously than over any other appointments. The lessons of Fortas, Haynsworth, Carswell, Bork, Ginsburg and Miers from the past 40 years or so, should warn presidents that they cannot appoint whomever they wish.

The justice must turn out as expected

Presidents can have a vacancy to fill, appoint someone whom they believe will change the judicial philosophy of the Court to their liking, and get them confirmed by the Senate, but if that justice does not turn out to be the kind of justice they originally believed, then the game is lost. And, as we have already hinted, some justices 'evolve', or maybe they were never what the president thought they were in the first place. Life tenure on the Supreme Court can lead to a worrisome degree of independence.

Let's look back at Table 2.2. We have said thus far that only two, maybe three, recent appointments to the Supreme Court have been what we might call game-changers — liberals for conservatives or vice versa. But there are two examples in that table of presidents who thought they were appointing game-changing justices but turned out to be hopelessly wrong.

The first was President Gerald Ford in 1975 in appointing John Paul Stevens to replace the liberal justice William Douglas, appointed by FDR in 1939. Here is what Ford writes in his autobiography, *A Time To Heal*, about the Stevens appointment:

> The Attorney General gave me a dozen suggestions. We asked legal scholars to read the candidates' opinions as jurists or their writings as members of the bar. Soon the list was down to five or six names…The final choice was between two men: Judge Arlin Adams and Judge John Paul Stevens. Both had received excellent ratings from the American Bar Association; both had had distinguished careers. I pored over their legal opinions myself. Stevens's opinions were concise, persuasive and legally sound. It was a close call, but I selected Stevens, and the Senate confirmed him by a vote of 98 to 0.

The trouble was, Ford thought he was appointing a conservative justice, thereby changing the balance of the Court to his liking — a conservative for a liberal. As a judge on the Seventh Circuit Court of Appeals (1970–75), Stevens had indeed had a moderately conservative voting record. And in his early years on the Supreme Court, Justice Stevens seemed still to hold to that path. He voted to restore the death penalty in the United States, and in the famous *Regents of the University of California* v *Bakke* case (1978), Stevens joined conservative justice William Rehnquist in opposing the racial quota programme at issue. But as the Court moved more to the right in the 1980s, Stevens moved to the left and spent much of the next three decades handing down decisions that were unashamedly liberal. In 2000, Stevens joined the Court's 5–4 majority to strike down a Nebraska state law banning the partial-birth abortion procedure. In 2005, he was again a member of the Court's 5–4 majority in *Roper* v *Simmons*, which held that convicted felons who had been under 18 when they committed their crime could not get the death penalty. These are just two recent examples of the liberal voice of Justice Stevens on the Supreme Court. There are countless others.

The second example of a president getting it wrong, so to speak, was President George H. W. Bush's appointment in 1990 of David Souter to replace liberal justice William Brennan. Brennan had been a thorn in the side of Republican presidents from Nixon to Bush, and Bush did not intend to put someone of Brennan's judicial philosophy on the Court to replace him. But he did not want another red-blooded fight like that which had erupted when President Reagan had tried to get Robert Bork on the Court in 1987. So Bush needed a conservative who could be his 'stealth candidate'. That was David Souter. But so little was known about Souter that even conservatives became a little concerned, and the Bush White House was happy to lay their fears to rest. Souter came from New Hampshire — the state of which White House chief of staff John Sununu had been governor. Tinsley Yarbrough, writing in *The Bush Presidency* (Macmillan, 1994), states:

> Sununu and other White House staffers assured conservatives…that Souter would keep the conservative faith on abortion and other controversial matters. 'There were no words exchanged that would constitute any specific assurances on any specific issue,' a staffer for a conservative lobbying group related in a confidential memo summarising his conversation with the White House Chief of Staff, 'but the general thrust of the discussion definitely made me feel better.'

Souter's nomination became something of a byword for conservatives. During the administration of President Bush's son, George W. Bush, opponents of Harriet Miers, about whom similarly little was known, were sporting lapel badges which read: 'No More Souters'.

But David Souter spent the next 19 years on the Court — until his retirement in 2009 — siding with the Court's liberal wing. His predecessor, Justice Brennan, would have been much happier with Justice Souter's record than would President Bush. At times, it is almost as if Supreme Court justices take on the mantle of their predecessor — a kind of 'Elijah effect'. (In the Old Testament — 1 Kings, chapter 2 — upon his translation to heaven, the prophet Elijah leaves his mantle (cloak) for his successor, Elisha. Later it was said that 'the spirit of Elijah doth rest on Elisha' (1 Kings, 2 v. 15, KJV).)

Both Ford in 1975 and Bush in 1990 had the opportunity of changing the political balance of the Court: a vacancy occurred; the nominee was thought to be of a different judicial philosophy from their predecessor; the Senate voted to confirm — all the first three criteria applied. But the justice did not turn out as expected.

Conclusion

It seems clear from the history of Supreme Court appointments over the past 35 years that it is exceedingly difficult for a president to change the political balance of the Court. Four different sets of requirements have to fall into place for this to occur and the chances of this are not especially high. We have discovered that between 1975 and 2009, only two presidents — both presidents Bush — have been able to shift the Court in this way. With their respective appointments of Clarence Thomas and Samuel Alito, each was able to shift the Court in a conservative direction.

So what about President Obama? We have seen that his first two Supreme Court appointments, Sonia Sotomayor in 2009 and Elena Kagan in 2010, are unlikely to change the Court's political balance. The only way President Obama can hope to change the Court's political balance is to appoint a liberal for a conservative. The trouble is that most of the Court's conservatives are currently the younger members of the Court — the least likely, therefore, to retire or die. As Table 2.3 shows, three of the five youngest members of the Court are conservatives and there is a significant age difference between these five justices and the other members of the Court. Thomas, the fifth most senior member of the Court by age, is 10 years younger than Stephen Breyer — the fourth most senior by age — although he joined the Court 3 years before Breyer.

President Barack Obama

| Table 2.3 | Birth dates and ages of Supreme Court justices |

Justice	Date of birth	Age (on 31/12/2010)
Ruth Bader Ginsburg	15 March **1933**	77
Antonin Scalia	11 March **1936**	74
Anthony Kennedy	23 July **1936**	74
Stephen Breyer	15 August **1938**	72
Clarence Thomas	23 June **1948**	62
Samuel Alito	1 April **1950**	60
Sonia Sotomayor	25 June **1954**	56
John Roberts	27 January **1955**	55
Elena Kagan	28 April **1960**	50

Liberal justices in blue   Conservative justices in red   Swing justice in black

Obama's best chance of nudging the Court to the left would be if either Justice Antonin Scalia's or Justice Anthony Kennedy's seat on the Court were to become vacant. Both celebrated their seventy-fourth birthday in 2010. If Obama were to be able to replace either Scalia or Kennedy with a liberal justice, then he might achieve what few of his recent predecessors have managed to do — to change the Supreme Court's political balance. The trouble is that Justice Scalia — a thoroughbred conservative — is unlikely to retire during Obama's presidency, knowing that he might be replaced by a justice more liberal than himself. The same might also be true of his fellow Reagan appointee, Anthony Kennedy. So the short answer to our question is probably — 'with great difficulty'.

Task 2.1

Source A is adapted from George C. Edwards, *Governing by Campaigning: The Politics of the Bush Presidency* (Pearson Longman, 2007). He is writing about President George W. Bush's nomination of Harriet Miers to the Supreme Court in 2005. Read Source A and then answer the questions that follow.

Source A

[Following the confirmation of Chief Justice John Roberts,] attention immediately turned to the President's nomination of White House counsel Harriet Miers to replace Justice O'Connor. Because Miers was largely unknown outside the White House, it appeared that Bush and his advisors had concluded that he could ill afford a bruising ideological fight over a Supreme Court nominee at a time when he and his party were besieged by problems. Bush apparently thought Miers' lack of a published record would make it easier to push her nomination through. What looked like a clever political decision soon turned sour, however.

Many of his most passionate supporters on the right had hoped and expected that he would make an unambiguously conservative choice to fulfil his goal of clearly altering the Court's balance, even at the cost of a bitter confirmation battle. By settling instead on a loyalist with no experience as a judge and little substantive record on abortion, affirmative action, religion, and other socially divisive issues, the President shied away from a direct confrontation with liberals and in effect asked his base on the right to trust him on his nomination. Many conservatives were bitterly disappointed and highly critical of the President. They demanded a known conservative and a top-flight legal figure.

The White House was surprised at the intensity of conservatives' anger and their irritation at not being given adequate warning that Miers was the President's choice. At first, it tried to pacify them by stressing Miers' conservative religious beliefs. But when liberals criticised the White House for cynically reversing its contention that John Roberts' religion was irrelevant to his confirmation, the White House tried to refocus the debate on to her legal qualifications.

The nomination had additional problems. It smacked of cronyism, with the President selecting a friend and a loyalist, rather than someone of obvious merit. Bush had handed his critics additional ammunition that he was prone to stocking the government with cronies rather than individuals selected solely for their qualifications.

In short order Miers withdrew from consideration, and the President nominated Samuel Alito a few days later. Alito was a traditional conservative and response to him followed party lines. The Senate confirmed Alito by a vote of 58–42.

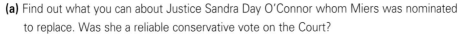

Task 2.1 (continued)

(a) Find out what you can about Justice Sandra Day O'Connor whom Miers was nominated to replace. Was she a reliable conservative vote on the Court?

(b) What reasons does Professor Edwards suggest for why the president did not at first nominate a known conservative judge to replace O'Connor?

(c) Why did Harriet Miers withdraw from consideration?

(d) Find out what you can about Justice Samuel Alito who eventually replaced Justice O'Connor? Has he thus far been a reliable conservative vote on the Court?

(e) What can you therefore conclude about the consequences of the Alito for O'Connor switch?

Guidance

(a) To find out more about Justice O'Connor's judicial philosophy, type the phrase 'Sandra Day O'Connor judicial philosophy' into an internet search engine (e.g. Google). This should bring up a number of useful sites for you to consult.

(b) Notice here that the president, presented with an opportunity to shift the balance of the Supreme Court, initially seemed to shy away from this.

(c) Think about who was opposing Miers' nomination. Does opposition to Supreme Court nominees usually come from the president's own supporters?

(d) Again, to find out more about Justice Alito's judicial philosophy, type the phrase 'Samuel Alito judicial philosophy' into an internet search engine.

(e) Refer to actual decisions mentioned in this chapter in which Justice Alito has taken a position different from that which Justice O'Connor might have taken.

Task 2.2

Source B is adapted from Lou and Carl Cannon's book, *Reagan's Disciple: George W. Bush's Troubled Quest for a Presidential Legacy* (Public Affairs, 2008). Read Source B and then answer the questions that follow.

Source B

By the time the Roberts Court ended its first full term on 28 June 2007, its direction was no longer in doubt. A series of rulings, all by 5–4 margins, had made it more difficult for workers alleging job discrimination to sue their employers, had declared unconstitutional on free speech grounds a section of the 2002 McCain–Feingold campaign finance law that had restricted political advertising, and had limited the power of school boards to use race as a tool for maintaining or achieving diversity. As Joan Biskupic, the Supreme Court reporter for *USA Today*, summarised the term: 'Roberts, fulfilling the conservatism inspired by his personal hero, Ronald Reagan, [took] command of the bench in a way that eluded his predecessor, the late William Rehnquist.' For the first time in more than half a century, conservatives had a Court they could call their own.

Task 2.2 (continued)

But whether this signifies a Roberts revolution remains to be seen. Certainly, this is what the Court's liberal minority fears. Perhaps, but what the Roberts Court has actually accomplished to date falls short of the claims on either side. For one thing, the change in judicial direction has been less than uniform and is arguably liberal on some issues. On 2 April 2007, for example, the Court held that the Environmental Protection Agency has the authority to regulate carbon dioxide and other emissions under the Clean Air Act. The Court, in a 5–4 decision hailed by environmentalists and deplored by the Bush administration, said motor-vehicle emissions make a 'meaningful contribution to greenhouse gas emissions' and therefore global warming.

Another reason for scepticism about the extent of the Roberts revolution is that some of the Court's most important decisions came with qualifications attached. The decision upholding the Partial Birth Abortion Act, for instance, did not even ban all late-term abortions, let alone reverse *Roe v Wade*.

As this is written in the aftermath of the Supreme Court's 2006–07 term, it is impossible to know if the conservative judicial revolution is at high tide or just beginning. Time is seemingly on the conservatives' side, as the average age of the four conservative justices is 13 years less than the average age of the four liberal justices. The bigger reason for judicial conservatives to be upbeat, at least in the short run, is that they hold a tactical advantage over the liberals. Unlike the situation on the Rehnquist Court (1986–2005), where conservatives needed the votes of both O'Connor and Kennedy to prevail, they now need only Kennedy's. In the 19 cases decided along ideological lines in the first full term of the Roberts Court, Kennedy was always in the majority. He sided with the conservatives in 13 of these cases and with the liberals in 6. As Justice Kennedy goes, so goes the Court, and this is why the Roberts Court is sometimes called 'the Kennedy Court'.

(a) What evidence do the authors present for the appointment by President Bush of John Roberts and Samuel Alito having turned the Court in a more conservative direction?

(b) What evidence do they present, however, for a more cautious view of the direction of the Roberts Court?

(c) What events in the future do you think might further change the Court's direction?

Guidance

(a) Focus on the material presented in the first paragraph of Source B.

(b) Focus on the material presented in the second and third paragraphs of Source B.

(c) You will want to consider: the material presented in the fourth paragraph of Source B; the balance between Republican and Democrat appointees currently on the Court; the likelihood of more Democrat-appointed justices; the likelihood of liberal-for-conservative appointments to the Court.

3 Can the Supreme Court 'amend' the US Constitution?

Of course, the obvious answer is that it cannot. Only Congress and the states can formally amend the US Constitution. The amendment process was all carefully written into the original Constitution in Article V. Constitutional amendments can be proposed either by Congress or by a national constitutional convention. In the former process, Congress must propose a constitutional amendment by a two-thirds majority in both houses of Congress. In the latter process — never used — a national constitutional convention called by at least two-thirds of the states would propose an amendment. Congress has successfully proposed a constitutional amendment on 33 occasions since 1787.

Once proposed, the amendment must then be ratified. Again there are two processes — either by state legislatures or by state constitutional conventions. In the former process, three-quarters of the state legislatures must vote to ratify the amendment. This has been used successfully for 26 amendments. In the latter process, three-quarters of the states must hold a constitutional convention and vote to ratify. This has been used successfully for just one amendment — the Twenty-First Amendment, which repealed the Eighteenth Amendment, thus ending the constitutional ban on alcohol. Thus there have been 27 successful attempts to amend the US Constitution, and none of them involved the US Supreme Court.

But what we have just explained is the *formal* process of constitutional amendment — the changing of the words. What the question asked in this chapter alludes to is what might be described as the *informal* process of constitutional amendment — the changing of *the meaning* of the words. Former Chief Justice Charles Evans Hughes famously remarked that Americans are 'under a Constitution, but the Constitution is what the judges say it is'. By this, Chief Justice Hughes was referring to a consequence of the Court's power of judicial review — the power to declare Acts of Congress or of state legislatures, or actions of the federal or state executives, unconstitutional. In declaring legislation or actions unconstitutional, the Supreme Court is, in effect, telling us what the Constitution means today — what phrases within the Constitution, mostly written in the eighteenth century, mean today in the twenty-first century.

'Originalism' v 'living Constitution'

But before we get to answer the question, we need to say something about the two views which exist on what the role of the Supreme Court should be when deciding such cases. We have so far referred to justices as being either 'strict constructionist' (or conservative), or 'loose constructionist' (or liberal). But there is another pair of terms we can use which is particularly relevant to the debate concerning the role of the Supreme Court in 'amending' the Constitution: 'originalists' on the one hand, and those who believe in a 'living Constitution' on the other.

Originalists believe that the Constitution has a meaning which is both known and fixed. It is the meaning that was intended when the Article or Amendment was originally written — hence the term 'originalists'. Justice Antonin Scalia, appointed to the Court by President Reagan in 1986, considers himself an orginalist. Here is Justice Scalia discussing this matter at a conference in Washington DC in March 2005:

> I am one of a small number of judges who are known as originalists. Our manner of interpreting the Constitution is to begin with the text, and to give that text the meaning it bore when it was adopted by the people. I'm not a 'strict constructionist'. I don't think the Constitution should be interpreted either strictly or sloppily; it should be interpreted reasonably. This is such a minority position in modern academic and in modern legal circles that on occasion when I've given a talk like this I'm asked a question from the back of the room — 'Justice Scalia, when did you first become an originalist?' — as though it is some kind of weird affliction that seizes some people — 'When did you first start eating human flesh?'

To Scalia and others like him, it is not the job of the Supreme Court to 'read things into' or 'find' things which are not in the Constitution. He pleads not guilty to the charge that originalists are inflexible, claiming:

> My Constitution is a very flexible Constitution. You want a right to abortion? Create it the way all rights are created in a democracy, pass a law. The death penalty? Pass a law. That's flexible.

In other words, Justice Scalia would argue that he is not against abortion rights for women, but that 'reading them into' the text of a Constitution that does not mention abortion rights is not the way to achieve them. It is the job of legislators to legislate, not judges. That is why Scalia and fellow conservatives describe the Court's announcing a woman's right to an abortion as 'legislating from the bench'.

Former Justice John Paul Stevens, appointed to the Court by President Ford back in 1975, saw things quite differently. His emphasis was on the Constitution as a living document whose interpretation should be shaped by 'the needs of the moment' and not simply frozen in time. Anyway, argued Stevens, can one always know exactly what the framers of an Article or Amendment actually meant at the time? In a recent interview, Stevens referred to a 2005 freedom of religion First Amendment case in which the Court decided about the meaning of the so-called Establishment Clause — 'Congress shall make no law respecting an establishment of religion'. Stevens commented:

> It is our duty to interpret the First Amendment not merely by asking what those words meant to observers at the time of the founding, but instead by deriving from the Establishment Clause's text and history the broad principles that remain valid today.

It is here that we can see the great divide between originalists and those who favour a living Constitution. The latter, of which Justice Stevens was an example, would argue that the Constitution gives principles that remain valid, but they must be shaped and applied to the changing realities that the Founding Fathers could not have conceived. Thus, while historical investigation can help us clarify what those principles were, it cannot in Stevens' view tell us how the text is to be applied today. To freeze the meaning of the Establishment Clause, for example — or any other part of the Constitution — in the understanding of those who wrote it, maybe 220 years ago, would be to put the Constitution in a straitjacket. For those who hold on to a belief in the Constitution as a living document, the role of the Supreme Court is to apply the original principles in the light of the 'evolving standards of decency' that mark a maturing society. Put more simply, the Court interprets a *never-changing* Constitution for an *ever-changing* society. Because the living constitutionalists have so often held the majority opinion in the modern Court over the originalists, there are numerous examples of where the Court has, as it were, 'amended' the Constitution.

The First Amendment

One of the parts of the Constitution which is the subject of frequent interpretation by the Court is the First Amendment:

Congress shall make no law respecting an establishment of religion, or prohibiting the free exercise thereof; or abridging freedom of speech, or of the press; or the right of the people peaceably to assemble, and to petition the Government for a redress of grievances.

It all sounds very grand, but what do those phrases, written in 1791, mean in today's America? We shall consider separately two of the freedoms addressed in this Amendment — freedom of religion and freedom of speech.

Freedom of religion

The opening 16 words of the First Amendment present the Supreme Court with something of a conundrum. How do you both prohibit the 'establishment of religion' (commonly known as the Establishment Clause) while at the same time not 'prohibiting the free exercise thereof' (commonly known as the Free Exercise Clause)? It is a puzzle with which the Court has grappled ever since the passage of the First Amendment in 1791. For most of the nineteenth and early twentieth centuries, the courts allowed a great deal of 'religion' in public life, and especially in schools. But more recently, in the view of many Americans, the Court has been more diligent in focusing on the first of these two phrases and less mindful of the second.

Back in the early 1960s, the Supreme Court — in the case of *Engel* v *Vitale* (1962) — decided that to 'make no law respecting an establishment of religion' meant not allowing, for example, the New York Board of Regents who ran public (i.e. state-run) schools in New York to compose a prayer for use in its schools, even if students were allowed not to participate. Writing for the majority in this case, Justice Hugo Black stated:

When the power, prestige and financial support of the government is placed behind a particular religious belief, the indirect coercive pressure upon religious minorities to conform to the prevailing officially approved religion is plain.

The lone dissenter in this case, Justice Potter Stewart, accused the majority of misconstruing the meaning of the First Amendment's religious clauses. His interpretation of them was this: that the Establishment Clause simply forbids the government from establishing an official church, and the Free Exercise Clause simply means that people cannot be coerced in matters of religious belief and practice. It was his understanding that the New York Board of Regents was infringing neither of these restrictions. The *Engel* decision brought a hostile response from religious, southern conservatives. South Carolina Democrat Mendel Rivers famously accused the Court of 'legislating — they never adjudicate — with one eye on the Kremlin and the other on the NAACP [National Association for the Advancement of Colored People]'. New York Republican congressman Frank Becker called the decision 'the most tragic ruling in the history of the United States.'

In subsequent years, other jurisdictions tried to discover what exactly would and would not be permitted in terms of religious observance and practice in public schools. The answer seemed to be: 'not a lot'. Two years after the New York case, the Court made another First Amendment ruling regarding religion in public schools — *Abington School District* v *Schempp* (1964). It was as if the Court was saying 'we meant what we said'. The case revolved round a Pennsylvania state law that required ten verses of the Bible to be read at the start of each school day in the state's public schools. The Court declared the law unconstitutional because it violated the Establishment Clause of the First Amendment. The state had claimed that its practice was different from that in New York because it was not the author of what was being recited. The Court regarded this as completely immaterial. Justice Potter Stewart again offered the lone dissent.

These cases set the scene for a battle that has raged within the Court for the last four decades. In subsequent decisions, the Court ruled on such matters as a period of silent reflection in schools, prayer at school graduation ceremonies, Christmas displays in shopping malls, and the display of the Ten Commandments in courtrooms and public spaces. The Court found that pretty much all of these fell foul of the Establishment Clause of the First Amendment.

Only in one case — *Zelman* v *Simmons-Harris* (2002) — did the Supreme Court take a different view on the meaning of the constitutional right to freedom of religion. In this case, the Court upheld a school voucher programme in Cleveland, Ohio, giving financial aid to parents to allow them to send their children to religious or private schools. In December 2000, the Federal Court of Appeals had declared the Ohio programme to be unconstitutional because it had the 'effect of promoting sectarian [i.e. religious] schools' and thereby violated the Establishment Clause of the First Amendment. But the five-member majority of the Supreme Court disagreed. Writing for the majority, Chief Justice William Rehnquist stated:

> The question is whether Ohio is coercing parents into sending their children to religious schools, and that question must be answered evaluating all options Ohio provides Cleveland school children, only one of which is to obtain a [voucher] and then choose a religious school.

But what the Court was doing in all these cases was updating the phrases of the First Amendment, written in 1791, and trying to apply them to modern-day American society. The first 16 words of the First Amendment remain unchanged, but their meaning has been significantly changed by the decisions of the Supreme Court, and in that sense the Court has the power to amend the US Constitution interpretively.

Freedom of speech

The First Amendment goes on to guarantee what it calls 'freedom of speech', stating that this freedom shall not be 'abridged'. But what constitutes freedom of speech? Does one have the right to shout 'fire!' in a crowded theatre? Curiously enough, that much-used question is itself a misquotation from a Supreme Court decision — *Schenck* v *United States* (1919). This early twentieth-century case revolved around whether Charles Schenck and other members of the American Socialist Party had violated the 1917 Espionage Act, which prohibited the obstruction of military recruiting, or whether their anti-war pamphlets were protected by the First Amendment's right to free speech. In finding against Schenck and upholding the Espionage Act, Justice Oliver Wendell Holmes, writing for the unanimous majority in this historic case, argued in words that gave rise to not just one famous phrase, but two:

> The most stringent protection of free speech would not protect a man **falsely shouting fire in a theatre** and causing a panic. The question in every case is whether the words used in such circumstances are of such a nature as to create **a clear and present danger** that they will bring about the substantive evils that Congress has a right to prevent.

So in 1919, the Court ruled that the First Amendment did not cover Communist Party anti-war literature. Since then, the Court has turned its attention to more modern manifestations of free speech. Do limits on political campaign contributions and expenditure limit free speech? In *Buckley* v *Valeo* (1976), the Court decided that parts of the 1974 Federal Election Campaign Act did just that, and declared them unconstitutional. In *Rankin* v *McPherson* (1987), the Court upheld the free speech rights of Ardith McPherson after she had been sacked for remarking at her workplace, the day after the unsuccessful assassination attempt on President Reagan in 1981, 'If they go for him again, I hope they get him.'

Then there were the flag-burning decisions — *Texas* v *Johnson* (1989) and *United States* v *Eichman* (1990) — in which the Court struck down both a Texas state law (1989) and a federal law (1990) banning flag burning. Writing for the majority in the *Johnson* decision, Justice William Brennan wrote:

> If there is a bedrock principle underlying the First Amendment, it is that Government may not prohibit the expression of an idea simply because society finds the idea itself offensive or disagreeable.

One can be fairly sure that when the framers wrote the First Amendment, they did not have the protection of flag burning in mind. But the Supreme Court in the late twentieth century decided that is what it meant today, and by doing so, in effect, amended the Constitution.

In the 1997 case of *Reno* v *American Civil Liberties Union*, the Court extended the First Amendment protection of free speech to the internet when it declared unconstitutional the 1996 Communications Decency Act. The Court struck down the Act because of its vague phraseology, banning anything on the internet that was 'indecent' or 'patently offensive'. 'The First Amendment Goes Digital' proclaimed the *Washington Post* headline. Writing for the seven-member majority in the case, Justice John Paul Stevens stated:

> The Communications Decency Act (CDA) lacks the precision that the First Amendment requires when a statute regulates the content of speech. In order to deny minors access to potentially harmful speech, the CDA effectively suppresses a large amount of speech that adults have a constitutional right to receive and to address to one another.

In the 2002 case of *Watchtower Bible and Tract Society of New York Inc.* v *Village of Stratton, Ohio*, the Supreme Court sought to protect yet another set of free speech rights — the right to visit door-to-door in a neighbourhood. The small town of Stratton, Ohio, had passed a law requiring anyone visiting door-to-door to get a permit beforehand. The law was challenged by the Jehovah's Witnesses, whose members are renowned for their door-to-door visiting. Writing for the eight-member majority, Justice Stevens stated:

> It is offensive, not only to the values of the First Amendment but to the very notion of a free society, that in the context of everyday public discourse a citizen must first inform the government of [his or] her desire to speak to [his or] her neighbours and then obtain a permit to do so.

An area of First Amendment rights much in contention today is the area of what we call 'political speech'. This has become an even more vexed question following the restrictions placed on campaign financing by the 2002 Bipartisan Campaign Reform Act (BCRA) of 2002. In *McConnell* v *Federal Election Commission* (2003), the Court upheld the provisions of the Act and so rejected the argument of its opponents that in banning soft money — unregulated money given to political parties by individuals for grassroots organising, get-out-the-vote drives and issue adverts — the law stifled free speech and was therefore contrary to the principles of the First Amendment. Justice Antonin Scalia, writing for the minority in a 5–4 decision, complained:

> Who could have imagined that the same Court which, within the past years, has sternly disapproved restrictions upon virtual child pornography, tobacco advertising and sexually explicit cable [television] programming, would smile in favour upon a law that cuts to the heart of what the First Amendment is meant to protect: the right to criticise the government?

But 4 years later, in *Federal Election Commission* v *Wisconsin Right to Life* (2007), the Court struck down a key element of BCRA as being a violation of the free speech guarantee of the First Amendment. The Court struck down the Act's ban on business corporation and labour union sponsorship of television advertisements — unless they explicitly urge a vote for or against a particular candidate — in federal elections in the 30 days before a primary or 60 days before a general election. 'Discussion of issues cannot be suppressed simply because the issues may also be pertinent in an election,' wrote Chief Justice Roberts for the five-member majority.

Then, in 2010, the Court went even further. In *Citizens United* v *Federal Election Commission*, the Court struck down all limits on pre-election advertising, allowing even those ads that explicitly urged a vote for or against a candidate. It further ended a 63-year-old ban on corporations using money from their general funds to produce and run their own political campaign advertisements. Again it was a 5–4 ruling with the conservatives joined by swing justice Anthony Kennedy. Authoring the majority opinion, Kennedy had this to say about First Amendment freedom of speech:

> When government seeks to use its full power, including the criminal law, to command where a person may get his or her information or what distrusted source he or she may not hear, it uses censorship to control thought.

Thus, these phrases from the First Amendment have been 'amended' — updated — by the Court to apply to circumstances that would have been quite unforeseeable by those who wrote the Constitution.

The Second Amendment

The case of *District of Columbia* v *Heller* (2008) was the Supreme Court's great landmark decision on the meaning of the Second Amendment's right to 'keep and bear arms'. The case centred on a gun law introduced in Washington DC in 1976, which banned the ownership of handguns and required that shotguns and rifles be kept in the owner's home, unloaded and dismantled or bound by a trigger lock.

Writing for the Court's five-member majority, Justice Antonin Scalia stated:

> We hold that the District's ban on handgun possession in the home violates the Second Amendment, as does the prohibition against rendering any lawful firearm in the home operable for the purpose of immediate self-defence. [The Second Amendment] surely elevates above all other interests the right of law-abiding, responsible citizens to use arms in defence of hearth and home.

Scalia was joined by his fellow conservative justices — John Roberts, Clarence Thomas and Samuel Alito — as well as by 'swing' justice Anthony Kennedy.

Writing for the Court's dissenting minority, Justice Stephen Breyer claimed that the decision 'threatens to throw into doubt the constitutionality of gun laws throughout the United States', calling the decision a 'formidable and potentially dangerous' mission for the courts to undertake. He was joined by liberal colleagues John Paul Stevens, David Souter and Ruth Bader Ginsburg.

What does the Second Amendment actually say about the right to carry guns? The wording, as well as the punctuation, is curious:

> A well regulated Militia, being necessary to the security of a free State, the right of the people to keep and bear Arms, shall not be infringed.

So what does it mean? Is it a guarantee of a right to form 'a well regulated militia' — a *collective* right to keep and bear arms — or is it a guarantee of an *individual* right to 'keep and bear arms'? Liberals, Democrats and friends of the Brady Campaign to Prevent Gun Violence have taken the former view. Conservatives, Republicans and paid-up members of the National Rifle Association (NRA) have taken the latter view. And with the exception of a rather obscure ruling back in 1939 in the case of *United States* v *Miller*, the Supreme Court has pretty much kept out of the debate.

How did the justices arrive at such differing conclusions about the meaning of 27 words? First, we need to divide the Second Amendment into two clauses — what we might call the preface ('A well regulated militia, being necessary to the security of a free state') and the operative clause ('the right of the people to keep and bear arms, shall not be infringed.'). Justice Scalia for the majority concluded that the preface does not limit or expand the scope of the operative clause, but grants *to each individual* the right to bear arms, and this right is not a *collective* one linked to joining a militia. He drew attention to the fact that the First, Fourth and Ninth Amendments all refer to *individual* rights and not to collective rights 'exercised only through participation in some corporate body'. But Justice Stevens for the minority believed that the preface's mention of a well-regulated militia meant that the right to bear arms is tied to service in a militia. He pointed out that the majority were restricting the meaning of the Second Amendment by limiting it to 'law-abiding, responsible citizens'.

The two sides then went on to debate the meaning of the phrase 'to keep and bear arms'. Justice Scalia stated that 'the most natural reading of "keep arms" is to "have weapons"'. He believed that '"keep arms" was simply a common way [in the eighteenth century, when the Amendment was formulated] of referring to possessing arms, both for militiamen and everyone else'. But Justice Stevens took a different view:

> A number of state militia laws in effect at the time of the Amendment's drafting used the term 'keep' to describe the requirement that militia members store their arms at their homes, ready to be used for service when necessary.

For Justice Stevens, the term 'bear arms' was 'a familiar idiom meaning to serve as a soldier, do military service, fight' — as defined by the *Oxford English Dictionary*.

But what we saw in *District of Columbia* v *Heller* was another example of the Supreme Court 'amending' the Constitution by interpretation, for as a result of this judgment, the Court announced for the first time that the Second Amendment right to bear arms is an individual right — yet another example of the Court telling us what eighteenth-century words mean today in the twenty-first century, and in that sense another example of the Court's ability to 'amend' the Constitution.

The Eighth Amendment

Another much-debated part of the US Constitution has been the Eighth Amendment, which states briefly:

> Excessive bail shall not be required, nor excessive fines imposed, nor cruel and unusual punishments inflicted.

It is the last six words of this Amendment — the prohibition against 'cruel and unusual punishments' — that has been at the centre of the Court's attention since its landmark decision of *Furman* v *Georgia* in 1972. There seems little doubt that the framers of the Amendment back in the 1790s where just as comfortable with capital punishment as they were with slavery and an all-male electorate. They would not have dreamed that the methods of execution used in the 1970s, such as the electric chair — not that the concept of an electric chair would have meant much to an eighteenth-century constitutionalist — could constitute a 'cruel punishment'. But that is essentially what the Court decided in its 1972 decision. Not only, ruled the Court, was the method cruel, but the way in which executions were handed out was arbitrary and unfair — or, in the vocabulary of the eighteenth century, 'unusual'.

Indeed, if we look at death penalty decisions by the Court, we can clearly see how the Court is 'amending' the concept of 'cruel punishments' to keep in line with the accepted views of American society at any given time. In *Wilkerson* v *Utah* (1888), the Court had concluded that execution by hanging or firing squad — the most used of methods at the time — was passable by the Eighth Amendment, but that dissecting or burning alive would not pass constitutional muster with the Court. But 100 years later, the Court was not only outlawing the use of the electric chair but also declaring in 2002 (*Atkins* v *Virginia*) that execution of mentally retarded criminals was unconstitutional, as was the execution of those who committed their crimes when under 18 years of age — *Roper* v *Simmons* (2005).

In 2008, the Court was asked to rule on whether Kentucky's practice of execution by lethal injection constituted a 'cruel punishment'. The Court decided that it did not. However, in the opinion of justices Clarence Thomas and Antonin Scalia in this case (*Baze* v *Rees*), the arguments put forward by the majority were erroneous. They argued

An electric chair

that it was very clear from precedent-setting cases, such as *Wilkerson* v *Utah*, that 'an execution method violates the Eighth Amendment only if it is deliberately designed to inflict pain'. Judged under that standard, they argued that this was an easy case 'because it is undisputed that Kentucky adopted its lethal injection protocol in an effort to make capital punishment more humane, not to add elements of terror, pain or disgrace'.

Here again, therefore, the Court through its power of judicial review has updated — amended, as it were — the meaning of the Eighth Amendment ban on 'cruel and unusual punishments'. As in other areas of constitutional law, the

Supreme Court has tried to reflect an ever-changing society in the way it has reinterpreted the meaning of words now over 200 years old.

The Fourteenth Amendment

The Fourteenth Amendment dates from 1868, just 3 years after the end of the Civil War. It defines citizenship, restricts the power of the states in their relations with their inhabitants and, most importantly, forbids a state from depriving any person of life, liberty or property without due process of law, and from denying to any person the equal protection of the law. Since its enactment, it has caused extensive controversy over what the Framers intended and how the Supreme Court has applied it. The equal protection clause, for example, has been used by the Court to restrain racial segregation, to maintain fair apportionment for state legislative districts, to gain equal justice for the poor, and to gain equal treatment for women. But its most famous and controversial citing was probably in the 1973 decision of *Roe v Wade*. In what was one of the most important decisions made by the Supreme Court in the twentieth century, the Court interpreted the right of 'liberty' in the Fourteenth Amendment to encompass a woman's right to choose to have an abortion. The relevant part of the amendment is what is usually referred to as the Due Process Clause:

> ...nor shall any State deprive any person of life, liberty or property, without due process of law.

As we have already stated, the Fourteenth Amendment was passed as a consequence of the civil war. No one is seriously suggesting that the civil war was fought about the issue of abortion. Nothing could have been further from the minds of those who crafted this amendment than a woman's right to choose an abortion. Yet 105 years later, the Supreme Court used its interpretive powers to read that particular constitutional right into this Amendment. In the most crucial sentence of the 1973 landmark decision, Justice Harry Blackmun for the seven-member majority wrote:

> This right of privacy, whether it be founded in the Fourteenth Amendment's concept of personal liberty and restrictions upon state action, as we feel it is, or, as the District Court determined, in the Ninth Amendment's reservation of rights to the people, is broad enough to encompass a woman's decision whether or not to terminate her pregnancy.

In the years since the Court made this judgment, countless critics have argued that its basis was flawed. Given that restrictive abortion laws were typically enacted by state legislatures dominated by men and that the burdens of undesired pregnancy fall only on women, the Court could have treated this case as one of gender discrimination. The Court's failure to present its majority opinion on these grounds may have been a tactical mistake, for even many scholars supportive of abortion rights for women have been critical of the flaws in Justice Blackmun's argument about 'privacy', by which the Court literally discovered a new right in the Constitution. It is one thing to reinterpret the meaning of rights specifically granted by the Constitution, but it is altogether another to find new rights that are actually not in the Constitution's wording at all.

Conclusion

Therefore we have seen that, although the Supreme Court has no power to amend the Constitution in the sense of amending the words, what the Court can and does do is to 'amend' the Constitution by interpretation. The vague phrases and words of the Constitution — 'freedom of speech', 'cruel punishments' and 'liberty', for example — allow the Court to say what these words and phrases actually mean today. Had the Founding Fathers gone for a document made up only of very specific wording, the only way of amending the Constitution would have been by formal amendment. Had they, for example, listed all the punishments they considered 'cruel', then each time Americans had wanted to add another, only formal amendment would have done. But the brilliance and lasting nature of the US Constitution are founded on its frequent vagueness. And it is that vagueness which the Supreme Court has adapted through decades — even centuries — of change. In this sense, therefore, the interpretive amendment of the Supreme Court has been, in many ways, far more significant and important than the formal amendments initiated by Congress and ratified by the states. What remains unresolved, however, is the question of whether the Supreme Court *should* be acting in such a way: originalist justices like Antonin Scalia and Clarence Thomas would say that it should not. What we have discovered in this chapter is that it does.

Task 3.1

Source A is adapted from Kermit Roosevelt's *The Myth of Judicial Activism* (Yale University Press, 2006). Read this extract and then answer the questions that follow.

Source A

The standard argument for originalism is relatively straightforward. The Constitution gets its legal

Task 3.1 (Continued)

effectiveness from the approval of the ratifiers. When the original Constitution was ratified, and when amendments were added to it over the course of years, a particular meaning was enacted, and judges are not given authority to change that meaning. The role of a judge is to say what the Constitution *does* mean, not what it ought to mean. If change is needed, Article V sets out the procedure by which it can be amended. Allowing judges free rein to change the meaning of the Constitution to suit the perceived needs of the day takes sovereignty away from the American people and places it in the hands of an unelected judiciary. Adherence to original understanding, by contrast, prevents judges from imposing their own values.

Originalists thus argue that constitutional cases should be decided according to our best guess as to how the ratifiers would have decided them. Judges should protect a right to abortion, for example, only if the ratifiers would have agreed that it existed. Anything else, say originalists, is illegitimate, or 'activist'.

The conventional argument for the living Constitution focuses on the fact that conditions and attitudes have changed greatly since the framers' times. Living constitutionalists argue that the Constitution must be able to adapt to respond to current needs and problems rather than remaining frozen in time. Because the amendment process is so difficult and cumbersome, requiring a two-thirds majority in both the House and the Senate and then ratification by the legislatures of three-quarters of the states, living constitutionalists seem to view judicial modification of the Constitution with equanimity — a necessary evil, at worst. Without judicial changes, they say, states would still be allowed to segregate schools, ban inter-racial marriage, and exclude women from the practice of law, to give just a few prominent examples.

(a) Write a short paragraph in which you summarise the arguments put forward to support originalism.

(b) Write a short paragraph in which you summarise the arguments put forward to support the idea of a living Constitution.

(c) Can you see any flaws in these two sets of arguments?

(d) Which argument do you find more persuasive?

Guidance

(a) You need to focus on the first two paragraphs from Source A. The second quotation in this chapter by Justice Antonin Scalia, beginning 'My Constitution is a very flexible Constitution', is also relevant.

(b) You need to focus on the third paragraph from Source A. The quotation in the chapter by former Justice John Paul Stevens, beginning 'It is our duty to interpret...' is also relevant.

(c) In considering the arguments put forward by the originalists, it is worth asking questions such as:

• How easy is it to discover what the framers of the original Constitution or of later amendments actually meant?

Task 3.1 (Continued)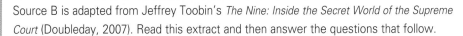

- Do you think they all wanted and meant the same thing?
- What would be the consequence for the Constitution in terms of the number of formal amendments if originalists had their way?

In considering the arguments put forward by those who support the idea of a living Constitution, it is worth considering such questions as:

- Does it give too much power to the Supreme Court?
- How accountable are the justices for their decisions?
- What if justices used this line of argument in a conservative rather than a liberal way (e.g. limiting freedoms rather than protecting and extending them)?

You will need to weigh the arguments put forward in (a), (b) and (c) as well as what you have read in this chapter. Try to give a reason for your conclusion.

Task 3.2

Source B is adapted from Jeffrey Toobin's *The Nine: Inside the Secret World of the Supreme Court* (Doubleday, 2007). Read this extract and then answer the questions that follow.

Source B

Justice Antonin Scalia's judicial philosophy was so clear and consistent, and his obligation to follow it so principled, that he could not bring himself to bargain with his colleagues. 'Originalists have nothing to trade!' he would say. 'We can't do horse-trading. Our view is what it is.' But originalism never caught on with anyone else on the Court, except with Justice Clarence Thomas. Justices like Sandra Day O'Connor, David Souter and Anthony Kennedy believed there was more to constitutional interpretation than just discerning the intent of the framers, including such factors as subsequent decisions of the Court, the expectations of the public, and the underlying values in the Bill of Rights, not just its text. In short, these justices believed in a 'living Constitution', a concept for which Scalia had nothing but contempt. 'A "living Constitution" judge', Scalia once explained, is a 'happy fellow who comes home at night to his wife and says, "The Constitution means exactly what I think it ought to mean!".'

Scalia thought *Roe* v *Wade* was the worst example of the living Constitution run amok. In his dissent in a later abortion rights case — *Planned Parenthood of Southeast Pennsylvania* v *Casey* (1992) — Scalia wrote:

> The issue in this case is whether the power of a woman to abort her unborn child is a 'liberty' protected by the Constitution of the United States. I am sure that it is not. I reach that conclusion not because of anything so exalted as my views concerning the concept of existence, or the mystery of human life. Rather, I reach it for the same reason I reach the conclusion that bigamy is not constitutionally protected — because of two simple facts: (1) the Constitution says absolutely nothing about it, and (2) the longstanding traditions of American society have permitted it to be legally forbidden.

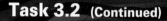

Task 3.2 (Continued)

(a) What does the author suggest justices who believe in a 'living Constitution' also consider in making their decisions, other than just the intent of the framers?

(b) What criticism does Justice Scalia make of this approach?

(c) Why does Scalia say he does not believe that abortion is a constitutionally protected right?

Guidance

(a) The material to focus on here is in the middle of the first paragraph.

(b) Look at the final sentence of the first paragraph.

(c) The material to focus on here is the Scalia quotation. Try to work out why Scalia also mentions that he would oppose bigamy (allowing men/women to have more than one wife/husband at the same time) for the same reason. What is society's general view of bigamy?

4 Has the Supreme Court effectively protected the rights and liberties of US citizens?

In answering this question we need to be careful to avoid a couple of pitfalls. The first is to presume that merely because the Supreme Court hears and decides cases regarding the rights and liberties of US citizens that it therefore, *per se*, protects them effectively. Activity does not always equal achievement. The second is that the understanding of what US citizens' rights and liberties are — even the understanding of who are fully regarded as US citizens — has changed significantly over the more than two centuries of the nation's history. To blame the Court for failing to uphold the rights of slaves in the 1850s would be rather like criticising Abraham Lincoln for writing the Gettysburg Address with a pen rather than using his personal computer: it is to attribute to the past the presumed benefits of the present.

The rights and liberties of US citizens are largely, though not exclusively, enumerated in the so-called Bill of Rights — the first ten Amendments to the federal Constitution, added in 1791. As we discovered in Chapter 3, the Supreme Court, through its power of judicial review, is called upon to say what the words — mostly written in the eighteenth century — mean today. As Chief Justice Charles Evans Hughes remarked in the early twentieth century, 'We are under a Constitution, but the Constitution is what the judges say it is.' It is this power which gives to the Court the role of protector of Americans' rights and liberties, for it is the justices who say what is meant by freedom of speech, freedom of religion, the right to bear arms, or whatever.

If the question had been, '*Does* the Supreme Court effectively protect the rights and liberties of US citizens?' we would need to consider only those cases of the very recent past, for it would be a question about current practice, about today. But the question we have posed is slightly more complex: '*Has* the Supreme Court effectively protected the rights and liberties of US citizens?'

It is, therefore, a question that calls for rather more of a historical perspective than we are used to giving. Not that the present-day is not relevant, it clearly is, but we need to see how the Court has performed in its role as protector of rights and liberties over a longer period of time. We cannot, of course, consider the Court's role in upholding all rights and liberties, so we shall concentrate on just three: race, abortion and freedom of religion.

Racial discrimination

To assess the effectiveness with which the Supreme Court has protected the rights and liberties of racial minorities in the USA, we shall consider seven landmark decisions of the Court spanning almost 150 years: *Dred Scott v Sandford* (1857), *Plessy v Ferguson* (1896), *Brown v Board of Education of Topeka* (1954), *Regents of the University of California v Bakke* (1978), *Richmond v J. A. Crosson Co.* (1989), *Gratz v Bollinger* (2003) and *Grutter v Bollinger* (2003).

Dred Scott **v** Sandford

The case of *Dred Scott v Sandford* holds a unique place in American constitutional history as an example of the Supreme Court trying to impose a judicial solution on a political problem. The ruling, which helped precipitate the Civil War, has long been considered one of the Court's great self-inflicted wounds. The question in the *Dred Scott* case was simply this: could a negro, whose ancestors were imported into the country and sold as slaves, become a member of the political community formed and brought into existence by the US Constitution, and as such become entitled to all the rights and privileges guaranteed in the Constitution to every citizen?

Dred Scott was born a slave and had been taken by his master to the free state of Illinois and then into that part of the 'unorganised territory' north of the line of latitude 36°30′ where slavery was forbidden by the Missouri Compromise of 1820. This was the compromise that prohibited slavery in the new territories and states north of the line which marked the border between Arkansas and Missouri (latitude 36°30′), but which admitted Missouri as a slave state, although it lay north of that line (see Figure 4.1). Upon his master's death, Scott argued that he was a free man — 'once free, always

A contemporary painting of Dred Scott (1795–1858)

free' — and sued for his freedom in the federal courts. But the case became a question not about Dred Scott's freedom, but about whether he had the right to sue in court if he was still a slave, for as a slave he had no legal standing. The Supreme Court ruled that as Scott was still a slave, he could not become a US citizen, and therefore he had no legal standing before the Court. That should have been the end of the matter.

Figure 4.1 The division between slave and free states as agreed by the Missouri Compromise, 1820

Source: http://faculty.umf.maine.edu

But Chief Justice Taney and the four Southerners among the eight associate justices on the Court at this time decided to go further, hoping that they could settle once and for all the issue of slavery in the new territories. Indeed, one of the associate justices, John Catron, had been put up to this by President-elect James Buchanan, who hoped thereby to unite the Democratic Party. The ruling, delivered just 2 days after Buchanan's inauguration, went on to declare the 1820 Missouri Compromise unconstitutional. Indeed, so much were the president and the Court in collusion that Justice Catron had informed Buchanan in advance of the decision the Court would announce, so that Buchanan could slip a reference about it into his inaugural address. The effect of declaring the Missouri Compromise unconstitutional was to open up the entire United States to slavery, hence the Civil War which erupted just 4 years after the Court's judgment. As Morison and Commager remark in their scholarly work, *The Growth of the American Republic* (1969):

Poor, foolish Buchanan! He had hoped for a peaceful term of office, but the Dred Scott case unleashed the worst passions of pro- and anti-slavery when his administration was less than a week old. By its ruling, the Court had sanctioned [the] doctrine that [while] slavery was national, freedom was sectional.

In its *Dred Scott* decision, the Court clearly did nothing at all for the rights and liberties of negro slaves. It was much more concerned with protecting the property rights of the slave owners. American legal and constitutional scholars consider the *Dred Scott* decision to be the worst ever rendered by the Supreme Court. It took 4 years of civil war and the Thirteenth Amendment to the Constitution to undo it. Unfortunately, Dred Scott died in 1858 — too soon to reap the benefits of the changes which followed that Amendment.

Plessy v Ferguson

Forty years later (1896), the Court did little better in the celebrated case of *Plessy* v *Ferguson*, in which the Court upheld a state law of Louisiana that required railroad companies to provide 'equal but separate accommodations for the white and coloured races' and barred persons from occupying railway carriages other than those to which their race had been assigned. The case was little remarked upon at the time but came to be regarded as of great symbolic importance in the next six decades.

Writing for the seven-member majority, Justice Henry Billings Brown took the narrowest imaginable interpretation of the post-Civil War amendments, claiming, for example, that the Thirteenth Amendment applied only to actions whose purpose was to reintroduce slavery. He further argued that laws requiring separation of the races did not suggest that one race was inferior to another. Inferiority, according to Justice Brown, arose only because one race *chose* to perceive the laws in such a way. Thus *Plessy* established what became known as the 'separate but equal' doctrine — that the races could be provided with separate facilities, provided they were 'equal'. Justice Brown also stated that laws could not alter the long-established customs of society, so for the Court to mandate that the races be mixed would be futile in the face of such public opposition.

The one lone voice in dissent was that of Justice John Marshall Harlan, who had joined the Court in 1877 and served until his death in 1911 — the third-longest tenure on the Court at that time. Harlan's dissent would later support eloquent rejections of the 'separate but equal' doctrine and contained one of the great ringing phrases for which he is best known:

The white race deems itself to be the dominant race in this country. And so it is in prestige, in achievements, in education, in wealth and in power.

So, I doubt not, it will continue to be for all time if it remains true to its great heritage and holds fast to the principles of constitutional liberty. But in view of the Constitution, in the eye of the law, there is in this country no superior, dominant, ruling class of citizens. There is no caste here. **Our Constitution is color-blind**, and neither knows nor tolerates classes among citizens. In respect of civil rights, all citizens are equal before the law. The humblest is the peer of the most powerful. The law regards man as man, and takes no account of his surroundings or of his color when his civil rights as guaranteed by the supreme law of the land are involved.

'Our Constitution is colour-blind' — a phrase that would be repeated in Supreme Court judgments for a century and more, and is still used today, commanding the same mix of wonder and puzzlement. Here was the Court's first whisper of the guarantee that 'all citizens are equal before the law' — a guarantee of rights and liberties that 'takes no account of his surroundings or his colour'. In 1897, Harlan was a lone voice. Fifty-five years later, Harlan's views would carry the majority of the Court and result in a stunning over-turning of the *Plessy* decision.

Brown v Board of Education of Topeka

As the centenary of the Civil War approached, African-Americans were still regarded and treated as second-class citizens throughout the South, where segregation was very much the order of the day — in schools, public transport and other public facilities. Buses, trains, waiting rooms, lunch counters, movie theatres, restaurants, parks — even in many churches — the doctrine of 'separate but equal' held sway, although no one in government or the courts seemed to worry too much about the 'equal' part.

However, the conscience of many Americans had been disturbed by what the great Swedish sociologist Gunnar Myrdal called 'the American Dilemma' — the paradox of a commitment both to equality and to white superiority. Americans had also witnessed and been shocked by the effects of racism in Nazi Germany as well as being somewhat embarrassed by the still segregated nature of much of their armed forces when fighting alongside the integrated armies of their European allies in the Second World War. Thus the scene was set for a stunning breakthrough for the rights of African-Americans in the landmark decision of *Brown v Board of Education of Topeka* in 1954.

When Earl Warren, the Republican governor of California, was appointed Chief Justice by President Eisenhower in 1953, few would have thought him a likely champion of individual rights or minority rights. In 1942, he had been one of the leading advocates of the internment of West Coast Japanese-American citizens following the Japanese bombing of Pearl Harbor. As governor, he had opposed the reapportionment of the state's legislative districts — an action that would undoubtedly have benefited minority interests. Yet as Chief Justice, Warren now presided over the Supreme Court as it made what one his successors, William Rehnquist, would later call 'the most dramatic expansion of constitutional protections of individual liberty and minority rights'. And whereas in 1897 only one voice could be heard stating the case for the rights and liberties of the negro population, in 1954 the ringing phrases were not just those of a majority, but of a unanimous Court.

> Segregation of white and colored children in public schools has a detrimental effect upon the colored children. The impact is greater when it has the sanction of the law, for the policy of separating the races is usually interpreted as denoting the inferiority of the negro group. A sense of inferiority affects the motivation of a child to learn. Segregation with the sanction of law, therefore, has a tendency to [retard] the educational and mental development of negro children and to deprive them of some of the benefits they would receive in a racial[ly] integrated school system.

And then came the clarion call:

> We conclude that, in the field of public education, the doctrine of 'separate but equal' has no place. Separate educational facilities are inherently unequal. Therefore, we hold that the plaintiffs and others similarly situated for whom the actions have been brought are, by reason of the segregation complained of, deprived of the equal protection of the laws guaranteed by the Fourteenth Amendment.

The Supreme Court did not sweep away segregation and institute equality of opportunity for all in 1954, but it did make a giant leap for African-American mankind in the United States. The Court led the way, and bit by bit, presidents, the Congress, state governments and public opinion followed — admittedly somewhat slowly at times — in its wake. It is worth remembering that as recently as the 1940s, the Supreme Court itself had maintained segregated toilets for Court employees. In fact, Associate Justice Stanley Reed, who served from 1938 to 1957, once refused to attend the annual Christmas party at the Court when he learned that black staffers had been invited as well.

The Court followed up *Brown* with the enforcement of busing to achieve racial integration in *Swann* v *Charlotte-Mecklenburg Board of Education* in 1971 — another 9–0 decision. But as the years passed, the Court found itself drawn

A 'colored' drinking fountain in a streetcar terminal, 1939

into a different kind of debate — about the rights of the majority, of so-called reverse discrimination and the constitutional standing of affirmative action programmes.

Regents of the University of California v Bakke

In 1972, Allan Bakke, a 32-year-old white student wanted to be a doctor. He was one of 2,664 applicants for 100 places at the University of California Medical School at Davis. While 84 of these 100 places were filled by regular admissions, 16 places were reserved for students of minority races — African-Americans, Asians, Latinos, Native Americans and so on. The test scores and grades required for admission for these 16 places were not as stringent as those required for regular admission. Rejected twice by Davis Medical School, Bakke filed a lawsuit alleging racial discrimination on the basis that his test scores and grades were higher than those of students admitted to the 'reserved' places.

In *Regents of the University of California v Bakke*, the Supreme Court ruled that racially exclusionary preferences constituted a quota, and that such racial quotas were a denial of the Equal Protection Clause of the Fourteenth Amendment. The Court's judgment stated that the university could consider racial criteria as part of its admissions procedures so long as 'fixed quotas' were not used.

Richmond v J. A. Croson Co.

Since the *Bakke* decision in 1978, the Supreme Court has found itself having to decide on the constitutionality of a number of affirmative action programmes. Essentially, the Court has had to rule on whether advantaging certain societal groups inevitably leads to the disadvantaging of other groups. The other thorny issue over affirmative action is how long these schemes might run for.

After all, if the aim of affirmative action programmes is to lead to a more equal society, then, if they work as their supporters claim they do, after a certain length of time they ought to have achieved their aim and therefore be no longer necessary.

In 1983, the city council in Richmond, Virginia, enacted the Minority Business Utilization Plan. This scheme required businesses contracted to do work for the city to set aside 30% of their subcontracts for minority-owned companies. After losing a contract for installing stainless steel toilets at the city jail because it lacked the required minority subcontractors, the J. A. Croson Company sued the city, claiming a violation of the Equal Protection Clause. The Court agreed and struck down Richmond's programme as unconstitutional. Justice O'Connor wrote for the six-member majority. For O'Connor, there was no doubt that the programme contained a racial classification which disadvantaged whites. Wrote Justice O'Connor:

> The Richmond Plan denies certain citizens the opportunity to compete for a fixed percentage of public contracts based solely upon their race.

But was the Court ruling out all race-conscious programmes? No, not exactly. And although this is where the Court, some would argue, fudged the issue, it is an important fudge to understand, for the story of the Court's view of affirmative action programmes ever since has largely centred upon it. O'Connor and her five colleagues took exception to the Richmond 30% quota, not just because it was a quota, but because it had been put in place merely on the basis of some *general and historical view* of racial discrimination, not on the basis of a *specific and contemporary view* of racial discrimination in Richmond in the 1980s. The city, for example, had conducted no research on discrimination against minority-owned companies in Richmond. To O'Connor and her colleagues, this was a fatal flaw. O'Connor therefore continued:

> Nothing we say today precludes a state or local entity from taking action to rectify the effects of **identified** discrimination **within its jurisdiction** [emphasis added]. If the city of Richmond had evidence before it that nonminority contractors were systematically excluding minority businesses from subcontracting opportunities, it could take action to end the discriminatory exclusion.

So the redress of discriminatory practices against racial minorities had to be specific and targeted. That was to be the Court's standard in future judgments.

In the 1995 decision of *Adarand Constructors* v *Peña*, the Court took exactly the same line regarding federal affirmative action programmes. As Associate Justice Antonin Scalia put it in his opinion in *Adarand*: 'In the eyes of the government, we are just one race here. It is American' — echoes here of Justice Harlan's 'colour-blind Constitution' of a century and more before.

Gratz v *Bollinger* and *Grutter* v *Bollinger*

Jennifer Gratz was white and a well-qualified candidate for undergraduate admission to the University of Michigan. But she was first placed on a waiting list and then rejected. Barbara Grutter, one of nine children of a minister of the Calvinist Christian Reformed Church, also white, had scored 161 on her exam when she was applying to the University of Michigan Law School, a score that would easily have gained her admission had she been from a racial minority group. But Ms Grutter was likewise placed on a waiting list and then rejected.

In *Gratz* v *Bollinger*, the Court ruled (6–3) that the University of Michigan's affirmative action-based programme for undergraduate admissions was unconstitutional because it was too 'mechanistic'. All African-American, Hispanic and American-Indian applicants were automatically awarded 20 of the 100 points required to guarantee admission. Chief Justice Rehnquist, writing for the six-member majority, argued thus:

> Because the University's use of race in its current [undergraduate] admissions policy is not narrowly tailored to achieve [the University's] asserted interest in diversity, the policy violates the Equal Protection Clause…The Court finds that the University's current policy, which automatically distributes 20 points, or one-fifth of the points needed to guarantee admission, to every single 'under-represented minority' applicant solely because of race, is not narrowly tailored to achieve educational diversity.

'Not narrowly tailored' and 'automatic' — these were the stumbling blocks for the Michigan programme. And Rehnquist went on in his judgment to refer back to Justice Lewis Powell's argument in the *Bakke* case 25 years earlier:

> In Bakke, Justice Powell explained his view that it would be permissible for a university to employ an admissions program in which 'race or ethnic background may be deemed a "plus" in a particular applicant's file'. He emphasised, however, **the importance of considering each particular applicant as an individual** (emphasis added), assessing all of the qualities that individual possesses.

Most of the public comment in the run-up to these two cases treated them as a single controversy. But two justices, Sandra Day O'Connor and Stephen Breyer, saw them as being distinctly different. Whereas the undergraduate admissions programme treated all applicants of minority race as the same, the graduate admissions programme at the Law School evaluated each candidate individually. As O'Connor and Breyer considered the cases, this significant difference loomed large and both decided to deny *Gratz* but uphold *Grutter*. Thus in *Grutter* v *Bollinger* the Court ruled (5–4) that the University of Michigan's Law School admissions programme was constitutional because it was an individually tailored scheme.

For Justice Clarence Thomas — an African-American who had benefited more than any of his colleagues from affirmative action programmes in earlier life — his conservative ideology was deeply offended by any kind of preferential programme for racial minorities. To Thomas and his fellow conservative jurists, both Michigan schemes were 'a sham' and 'a naked effort to achieve racial balancing'. Thomas added his own colourful language to the dissenting minority opinion, describing racial diversity programmes as 'the faddish slogan of the cognoscenti' that do 'nothing for those too poor or uneducated to participate in elite higher education'. Thomas went on:

> What I ask for the Negro is not benevolence, not pity, not sympathy, but simply justice. The American people have always been anxious to know what they shall do with us…All I ask is, give him a chance to stand on his own legs! Let him alone!

Commented Jeffrey Toobin (*The Nine: Inside the Secret World of the Supreme Court*): 'For all its rhetorical power, Thomas's opinion represented only a fringe view — on the Court, and in the nation at large.' How things had changed in both the Court and the nation since Justice Harlan had expressed his 'fringe view' 109 years earlier. Harlan was now in the majority, and some! Thus we can see that over this period, the Supreme Court became more and more effective at protecting the rights and liberties of racial minorities, and in its later rulings on affirmative action it tried hard to tread the line between minority and majority rights.

Abortion

For the first half of the twentieth century, abortion was a taboo subject in America. It had not always been so. Back in the nineteenth century, abortions became quite common, but then the American Medical Association began an aggressive anti-abortion campaign, claiming the procedure was both morally wrong and medically harmful. The campaign was so successful that by 1910, every state in the Union had outlawed abortion. That is, of course, not to say there were no abortions. After-hours or back-alley abortions were available to those who could pay, as were mystery weekends away in Tijuana, just across the Mexican border. Many women died from botched operations.

In the second half of the twentieth century, civil liberty pressure groups — led by Planned Parenthood, the National Association for the Repeal of Abortion Laws (NARAL) and the American Civil Liberties Union (ACLU) — began to bring the topic out into the open once more. But many states were resistant to these groups' efforts to repeal their anti-abortion laws.

Norma Lee Nelson was a high school dropout, born of parents who divorced when she was 13. She married at 16 to a twice-divorced sheet metal worker, 'Woody' McCorvey, but he beat her up when he learnt she was pregnant and she ran away. Two-and-half-years later, in 1969, she was pregnant for a third time and this time sought an abortion. But to try and get the abortion she falsely alleged to have been the victim of a gang rape. A doctor she consulted put her in touch with a lawyer. The rest, as they say, is history. To protect her anonymity, she became Jane Roe for the purpose of the court case, and so by 1972, the case of *Roe* v *Wade* arrived at the Supreme Court. The Court announced its landmark decision the following year.

But we need to retrace our steps for a moment, for *Roe* v *Wade* was not the first case dealing with issues about procreation. It was actually the third. In *Griswold* v *Connecticut* (1965), the Court struck down a Connecticut state law that prohibited the use of contraceptives based on an implied constitutional right of privacy. Then in 1972, in *Eisenstadt* v *Baird*, the Court struck down a Massachusetts state law banning the sale of contraceptives. *Griswold* dealt with the rights of married people to use contraceptives. But *Eisenstadt* then extended this right to unmarried people. Justice William Brennan, writing for the majority, stated:

> If the right of privacy means anything, it is the right of the individual, married or single, to be free from unwarranted governmental intrusion into matters so fundamentally affecting a person as the decision whether to bear or beget a child.

This was a crafty move on Brennan's part. He added this wording to the opinion only after he had started his consideration of *Roe* v *Wade*. As Edward Lazarus (*Closed Chambers: The Rise, Fall, and Future of the Modern Supreme Court*) comments:

> Brennan knew well the tactic of 'burying bones' — secreting language in one opinion to be dug up and put to use in another down the road. *Eisenstadt* provided the ideal opportunity to build a rhetorical bridge between the right

to use contraception and the abortion issue pending in *Roe*. And taking full advantage, Brennan slipped into *Eisenstadt* the tendentious statement explicitly linking privacy to the decision whether to have an abortion.

In the opinion of Professor Kermit Roosevelt (*The Myth of Judicial Activism*), '*Roe* is a woefully unconvincing opinion', although 'there is a constitutional argument for protecting a woman's right to choose.' The *Roe* decision simply assumed that the Due Process Clause protects certain 'fundamental rights' unmentioned in the Constitution. Certainly the Court was seen by women's rights groups as the knight in shining armour, but the decision has something of 'the end justifying the means' about it. Associate Justice William Rehnquist, one of the two dissenters in the case, believed that such issues as abortion rights were 'far more appropriate to a legislative judgement than to a judicial one'. But whatever else is said, it had a profound effect on women's rights and on the availability — and thereby the frequency — of abortions.

But whereas the decision by the Court in *Brown* v *Board* back in 1954 clearly swung the argument about segregation decisively in one direction — to bring it to an end — *Roe* v *Wade* had no such unifying effect on the abortion debate, indeed quite the opposite: *Roe* v *Wade* remains one of the most polarising and divisive judgments in the history of the modern Court. People's views on *Roe* are almost a litmus test for their political ideology. No one today would think that asking a voter, a candidate for elective office, or a Supreme Court nominee for their views on *Brown* v *Board* would elicit much of interest. True, *Brown* v *Board* was not without criticism at the time. But today it is safe and secure in the constitutional structure of the country. As Professor Roosevelt states: '*Brown* has moved from a bitterly contested decision to an almost unassailable one.' In 1948, 6 years before *Brown*, Strom Thurmond ran for president on a platform of segregation and won four states. In 2002, when Senate Majority Leader Trent Lott suggested that the country would have been better off if Thurmond had won that election, Lott was forced to step down from his leadership post. It shows the extent to which the public view has changed.

But, as Figure 4.2 shows, there has been very little change in the public's views on abortion in the nearly 40 years since *Roe* v *Wade*. The majority view on abortion has consistently been that it should be legal but with certain restrictions. The two 'extreme' positions — 'no restrictions' and 'no abortions' — are, and always have been, strictly minority views.

As the number of abortions performed each year in the United States increased for some 17 years after this decision (see Figure 4.3), many state legislatures began to push the boundaries back to see what restrictions the

Court might permit to a woman's right to choose. Thus in 1992, the Court was faced with another landmark decision to make, a decision from which many observers thought *Roe* v *Wade* would not emerge intact.

In the 19 years since *Roe* v *Wade*, six justices had left the Court. What is more, these six retirees had all been in the seven-member majority in the case.

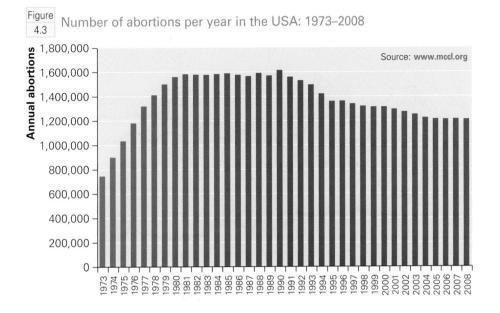

| Figure 4.2 | Public opinion on abortion in the USA: 1975–2008 |

Source: www.gallup.com

— Legal only under certain circumstances   — Legal under any circumstances   — Illegal in all circumstances   — No opinion

| Figure 4.3 | Number of abortions per year in the USA: 1973–2008 |

Source: www.mccl.org

Two of the three justices who remained from 1973 were the two dissenters, William Rehnquist and Bryon White. The only member of the majority opinion who remained was its author Harry Blackmun. The six retirees had all been replaced by nominees of Republican presidents — Stevens (Ford), O'Connor, Scalia and Kennedy (Reagan), plus Souter and Thomas (Bush). If ever *Roe* was going to bite the dust, it was probably going to be in 1992 in *Planned Parenthood of South-eastern Pennsylvania* v *Casey.* But that is not what happened.

Instead, justices O'Connor, Kennedy and Souter wrote an opinion that both reaffirmed a woman's constitutional right to abortion and set out two arguments why *Roe* should not be overturned. Their first reason was essentially that *Roe* was correct in fact, if somewhat weak in argument. True, it was difficult to justify a woman's right to choose from the right to 'privacy' — a right which the Constitution never mentions. But, according to this threesome, one could deduce it from the Fourteenth Amendment's protection of 'liberty'. And, according to O'Connor, Kennedy and Souter, the liberty protected by the Constitution extends to 'intimate and personal choices', of which abortion is one, and therefore the state may not place an 'undue burden' in the path of a woman seeking an abortion before the foetus is viable.

The second reason they came up with for not overturning *Roe* v *Wade* was *stare decisis* — the principle that the Court should generally not overrule

Anti-abortion cartoon from 2008 marking 35 years after Roe *v* Wade

previous decisions. The Court now held that *Roe* v *Wade* was a kind of special case in which the 1973 Court had tried to resolve an 'intensely divisive controversy'. In such circumstances, argued O'Connor, Kennedy and Souter, the Court would undermine its legitimacy if it reversed itself merely because new justices had been appointed since the previous decision.

On the day when the *Casey* decision was due to be announced, the Court's marble forecourt was overrun by television crews, microphones, dozens of police officers and crowds of both 'pro-choice' and 'pro-life' supporters shouting, and waving their appropriate signs — 'Keep abortion safe and legal' mingling with 'Abortion stops a beating heart 4400 times a day'.

In their *Casey* decision, the Court's fractured majority upheld various restrictions placed upon a woman's right to abortion by the Pennsylvania state legislature — she must receive counselling on the risks and alternatives, and she must wait 24 hours after receiving the counselling. Women under 18 had to gain parental consent. But the Court struck down the law's requirement that married women get the written permission of their spouse — a significant achievement by Justice Sandra Day O'Connor, who in her Opinion reminded the Court and the country that 'there are millions of women in this country who are victims of regular physical and psychological abuse at the hands of their husbands'.

Although some would suggest that the Court took a step back on women's rights when, in its 2007 decision of *Gonzales* v *Carhart*, the Court upheld the Partial-Birth Abortion Ban Act of 2003, the Supreme Court has undoubtedly been very effective in achieving for women what the Congress would and could not do — achieving a woman's right to choose whether or not to have an abortion. Some would state on moral and religious grounds that this constitutes regress not progress. But be that as it may, the Court has certainly fought effectively for that right which most Americans see as just — that abortion should be legal, under certain circumstances.

Freedom of religion

One of the most controversial areas of the Court's attempts to protect the rights and liberties of American citizens has been in the area of freedom of religion. This stems from what we refer to as the Establishment Clause in the First Amendment, which prohibits Congress from making any law 'respecting an establishment of religion'. But the amendment goes on to prohibit Congress from 'prohibiting the free exercise' of religion. These two parts of the First Amendment's Establishment Clause set up a potential and awkward contradiction.

According to Mark Levin (*Men in Black: How the Supreme Court is Destroying America*), the Supreme Court has, for American citizens, 'simply abolished your right to the free exercise of your religion in public'. It has done so, he suggests, in contradiction of 'the plain meaning of the religion clauses' and 'because it wishes to dictate policy'. Levin is therefore accusing the Court of being partial in its interpretation of the Establishment Clause and of exhibiting that trait of judicial activism — 'legislating from the bench'.

Before we analyse this claim by looking at some cases involving the Establishment Clause, we need to make ourselves aware of the background to this part of the Constitution. At the time of the ratification of the First Amendment in 1791, several states had established churches — in other words, they had an arrangement within their state similar to that which currently exists in England regarding the Church of England. The Establishment Clause was not put in to stop such arrangements. On the contrary, it was intended to protect state-established religion from federal government interference, hence the First Amendment states that '**Congress** shall make no law respecting an establishment of religion' (emphasis added).

But like other parts of the Bill of Rights, the First Amendment's Establishment Clause also had an individual dimension to it. It was not there just to protect the rights of American citizens *en masse*, but also *individual* citizens' rights. In the words of James Madison, it was there to ensure that Congress could not 'compel men to worship God in any manner contrary to their conscience'. But all these restrictions applied to Congress. That was because in the minds of the Founding Fathers back in the late eighteenth century, the threat to individual liberty would come not from the states but from that distant and somewhat distrusted national government.

Now turn the clock on to the 1860s and what Abraham Lincoln had spoken of in his Gettysburg Address as the 'new birth of freedom'. The amendments that came as a result of the Civil War changed the relationship between the federal and state governments significantly. Whereas the Founding Fathers had seen the federal government as the threat to liberty, now the framers of the Reconstruction Amendments saw the threat as coming from the states. So, just as in the Civil War itself, federal government intervention would be necessary to secure individual liberty in the states. And so the Fourteenth Amendment (1865) proclaimed that 'No state shall make or enforce any law which shall abridge the privileges or immunities of citizens of the United States.' From that point on, the individual states were bound to the Establishment Clause through the Fourteenth Amendment. That is why, by the time we come to the twentieth century, we have the Supreme Court arbitrating about *state laws* — not just those passed by Congress — conflicting with the First Amendment's Establishment Clause: thus the Supreme Court is having to act as umpire over the supposed 'wall of separation between church and state'. It is a role that the Court has found somewhat burdensome, as it stated with slight exasperation in the opening sentence of *Roemer* v *Maryland Public Works Board* (1976) with the line: 'We are asked once again to police the boundary between church and state.'

In a series of controversial decisions dating from the 1940s onwards, the Supreme Court: stopped the reimbursement of school travel costs to parents of children at Catholic schools (*Everson* v *Board of Education of Ewing Township* — 1946); declared unconstitutional a Christian prayer written for daily recitation in New York's public (i.e. state) schools (*Engel* v *Vitale* — 1962); banned devotional Bible reading and recitation of the Lord's prayer in public schools (*School District of Abington Township* v *Schempp* — 1963); forbad a period of 'silent reflection' in Alabama public schools (*Wallace* v *Jaffree* — 1985); banned a Christmas nativity scene in a county courthouse (*County of Allegheny* v *ACLU* — 1989) despite having upheld a 'seasonal' display of Santa, reindeers and the like in an earlier case; and struck down prayers at a Rhode Island school graduation ceremony (*Lee* v *Weisman* — 1992). And this is only a sample, not an exhaustive list. It is this list that would convince Mark Levin that the Court has abolished the rights of Americans to exercise their religion freely.

But we need to consider the other side of the coin. In making these decisions, the Court has been protecting the rights and liberties of those Americans who do not wish to see their tax dollars subsidising attendance at religious schools or nativity scenes, and who do not think that school is necessarily the most appropriate place for devotional Bible reading and prayer. Furthermore, the Court has, during the same period, made decisions that went the other way. In *Witters* v *Washington Department of Services for the Blind* (1986), the Court unanimously declared that giving state financial aid to someone who was training to be a minister of religion did not violate the First Amendment's Establishment Clause, as the Commission that made the grants gave them to any visually impaired person who wanted to become 'more productive members of society'. According to the Court, therefore, the grant scheme was 'neutral' in terms of religion.

Similarly, in the case of *Board of Education* v *Mergens* (1990), the Court found in favour of a religious group in a church-and-state case. Students at a public high school had been denied permission to hold a religious after-school club. But the Court found that the school's actions were unconstitutional because the school permitted non-religious clubs — such as chess, student government and community service — to meet after school. The Court disagreed with the school management's argument that, by permitting a religious after-school club, it would be endorsing the religious beliefs and practices of the group.

In the landmark decision of *Zelman* v *Simmons-Harris* (2002), the Court upheld a school voucher programme in Cleveland, Ohio, which resulted in parents using state-funded aid to send their children to private religious schools. The Court's five-member majority argued that Ohio was not 'coercing parents into sending their children to religious schools', but that this was 'only one option Ohio provides Cleveland school children'. Justice Souter disagreed, believing the scheme would 'force citizens to subsidise faiths they do not share even as it corrupts religion by making it dependent on government'.

Thus, upon closer scrutiny, it would appear that the Supreme Court has succeeded in walking a difficult tightrope between the two parts of the Establishment Clause — neither permitting an 'establishment of religion' nor 'prohibiting the free exercise thereof'. It might be argued that the Court has taken a rather more relaxed view of the 'separation of church and state' as the Court has become more conservative in its collective ideology following the appointments of associate justices Antonin Scalia, Anthony Kennedy and Clarence Thomas in the 1980s and 1990s. One might, therefore, also presume that this could continue with the addition of John Roberts and Samuel Alito in the last few years.

Conclusion

We have considered three important areas of civil rights and liberties in which the Court has been heavily involved over a number of decades. The question we are addressing concerned the effectiveness of the Court's protection of these rights and liberties. There is no doubt that, in considering the rights of racial minorities, the Court — reflective of American society as a whole — was slow to provide African-Americans with any protection of their rights and liberties. Indeed, it initially even denied them access to the judicial process by denying their citizenship. It then promoted 'separate but equal', the judicial impetus behind and endorsement of segregation. But come the 1950s, it was the Supreme Court that took the initiative — long before either of the other two branches of the federal government — to move the country towards desegregation and equality of opportunity. Then, as affirmative action programmes took effect, the Court balanced its watchfulness for minorities with a watchfulness for the majority, guarding against 'quotas' and 'reverse discrimination', striving towards that colour-blind Constitution of which Justice Harlan had spoken literally decades before.

We saw a similar balancing act in the matter of abortion. Initially, the Court announced a woman's right to choose (*Roe* v *Wade*) as being a constitutionally protected right — women's equivalent of *Brown* v *Board*, if you will. But then, as the decades passed, the Court balanced that with the restrictions which much of society deemed both necessary and proper to protect the life of the unborn. Thus, the Court has effectively protected the rights of both 'choice' and 'life'.

And finally, the Court has effectively protected both sides in the fierce debate over the separation of church and state. The Court has protected the rights of Americans who do not wish to see state organisation and promotion of religion, while still ensuring that those Americans who wish to exercise their faith in public are not discriminated against. The two decisions of *Engel* v *Vitale* and *Board of Education* v *Mergens* clearly show this two-pronged approach — the Court says no to state-written and state-imposed prayer in school, but says yes to voluntary religious practice after school.

On none of these three issues does the Court take a position that pleases any of the 'extremist' groups: it neither subjugates minority races nor imposes undue and unfair burdens upon those of the majority; it neither permits unlimited abortion nor bans abortion under any circumstances; it neither permits a free rein to religion in public life nor bans it. Not that the Court has always taken such a balanced view on these, or other, policy areas. But one can with some degree of accuracy say that, today — more perhaps than in the past — the Supreme Court does effectively protect the rights and liberties of American citizens. Maybe that is why the Supreme Court today is regularly held in much higher esteem than either of the other two branches of the federal government.

Task 4.1

Source A is adapted from Sandra Day O'Connor, *The Majesty of the Law: Reflections of a Supreme Court Justice* (Random House, 2003). In it, the former Associate Justice of the Supreme Court, who served from 1981 until her retirement in 2006, writes about the importance of the Court in protecting the rights and liberties of American citizens. Read Source A and then answer the questions that follow.

Source A

The Bill of Rights has permitted us to place the most essential individual liberties beyond the reach of the majority and to guard the individual against the excesses of government. Although our Bill of Rights is only a few pages long and has been in force for more than 200 years, great debates continue to rage over the proper meaning and implementation of its few words. But while we

Task 4.1 (Continued)

continue to dispute the exact meaning of the rights it guarantees, we agree that our law protects certain, basic rights from any governmental intrusion.

Governments must create a haven where citizens enjoy their constitutional and civil liberties in defiance of all the powers that the state or the masses can bring to bear. All these rights must be enforceable. In our system, it is the citizens themselves, through the courts, who enforce their rights. Enforcement is entrusted not to other government branches, agencies, or commissions that lack a personal stake in the aggrieved party's freedom but to the people. They take their claims to the courts, and the courts decide whether the actions of the executive or legislative branch have encroached upon some protected rights. The courts then have the power to halt the official conduct that violates those rights, and to order relief for past injury. Even in the Supreme Court where I work[ed], any person, regard-less of status, may file a petition — handwritten, if the petitioner lacks the resources for a more formal filing — and that petition will receive careful and thorough consideration.

Thus citizens turn to judges, who are empowered to invalidate the laws that encroach on protected rights. The courts may at times act in ways contrary to the will of the majority, but in so doing they further the principles of our system by ensuring that all groups, including outsiders and minorities, enjoy certain basic protections.

(a) From what does Justice O'Connor state Americans' basic rights are being protected?

(b) Why does O'Connor suggest that the courts are the most suitable branch of government for protecting rights and liberties?

(c) Why does O'Connor suggest that it is acceptable that the courts will 'at times act in ways contrary to the will of the majority'?

Guidance

(a) The answer comes at the end of the first paragraph. What do you think O'Connor means by this phrase?

(b) You need to focus both on the powers that the courts possess to protect rights and liberties as well as the reasons why the other branches of government would usually be less suitable to perform this task.

(c) The answer comes at the end of the final paragraph. Who else has rights in a democracy, other than 'the majority'? Does this also suggest another reason why Congress and the president will find it more difficult to act in this way?

Task 4.2

In January 2010, the Supreme Court declined to review a case in which the US appeal court upheld a high school dress code which banned students from wearing clothing that featured political comments. High School student Paul Palmer was banned by Waxahachie High School in Texas from wearing various T-shirts including one which had 'Freedom of Speech'

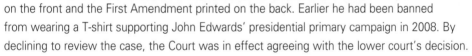

Task 4.2 (Continued)

on the front and the First Amendment printed on the back. Earlier he had been banned from wearing a T-shirt supporting John Edwards' presidential primary campaign in 2008. By declining to review the case, the Court was in effect agreeing with the lower court's decision.

Here's something interactive for you to try. Go to **www.ourcourts.org** which is a website supported by the former Supreme Court Associate Justice Sandra Day O'Connor. Having reached the home page, click on 'Play games' and then click on 'Supreme Decision' and follow the on-screen instructions. This is a simulation of how Supreme Court justices make decisions about individual rights. The example used is the right of a student to wear a certain T-shirt to school.

5 Is the Supreme Court a political institution?

In the year 2000, Americans went to the polls on 7 November to elect a new president. As the polls closed in most of Florida at 7 p.m. eastern standard time, the television networks began calling the state for the Democratic candidate, Al Gore. They coloured the state blue (for Democrat, as opposed to red for Republican) on their electronic maps, indicating that Gore would win all of the state's 25 electoral votes. Then by 8 p.m. the states of Michigan and Pennsylvania were coloured blue — another 41 electoral votes — and it was looking pretty certain that Vice-President Gore would hold the White House for the Democrats.

But a couple of hours later, after polls had closed in the Florida Panhandle — including the city of Pensacola — the television networks began, one by one, to retract their calling of Florida for Gore, indicating that the state was now 'too close to call'. In the small hours of Wednesday morning (8 November), the state was turned red, indicating the networks' belief that the state would be won by the Republican candidate, Governor George W. Bush. Then that was retracted, and the state was again declared 'too close to call'. It was not for another 35 days that the result in Florida — and with it the final result of the election — was finally decided. On Tuesday 11 December, exactly 5 weeks after Election Day, the US Supreme Court, in the case of *George W. Bush* v *Albert Gore Jr*, decided that no further recounting of votes should happen in Florida. The consequence of that decision, made by a 5–4 majority, was that Bush won Florida and with it the presidency.

In my courses on the US president, I had of course always taught my students that the president selects the members of the Supreme Court. Imagine my surprise when, in that year's election, the Supreme Court selected the president! Or that is what it appeared to do. Surely, never again, would one be able to say anything other than that the US Supreme Court is a *political* institution.

Whenever the word 'political' or 'politics' comes in the same sentence as 'court', one is tempted to react with considerable concern and disquiet. Allegations that a court has been 'politicised' or that judges are 'playing politics' rightly trouble those who believe that, in a liberal democracy, courts should be entirely separate from politics, lest their independence is compromised. But here is University of Texas law professor Lucas Powe writing in a recent book about the Supreme Court (*The Warren Court and American Politics*, 2002):

> All courts are political. The Supreme Court is a political body. It sits at the top of the third branch of government, whose ranks are filled with politically connected lawyers who regularly make influential decisions about important political matters.

So why is the Supreme Court sometimes thought of as a political institution? We shall consider seven reasons: first, the Court is appointed by a politician (the president); second, the Court is confirmed by other politicians (the Senate); third, the Court, through its power of judicial review, makes decisions in policy areas that are at the centre of political debate; fourth, the case of *Bush v Gore* in 2000; fifth, we often use the political terms 'conservative' and 'liberal' to refer to the justices; sixth, the Court also makes decisions that may either expand or limit the power of the president; finally, the Court — like other political institutions — is subject to democratic control and accountability, including a certain degree of influence from public opinion.

The nomination process

We have studied the nomination process in detail in Chapter 1, so all we need to do here is to focus briefly on the political nature of this process. We saw in Chapter 1 that presidential candidates often make the filling of Supreme Court vacancies an issue in their election campaigns. We saw that George W. Bush and Al Gore did this in 2000, as well as Barack Obama in 2008.

Once in office, presidents then try — not always successfully — to choose justices who reflect their own political and judicial philosophy. Democrats attempt to choose judges whom we describe as 'liberal' or 'loose construc- tionist'; Republicans hope to choose judges whom we describe as 'conservative' or 'strict constructionist'. Democrats Bill Clinton and Barack Obama chose liberals such as Ruth Bader Ginsburg, Stephen Breyer, Sonia Sotomayor and Elena Kagan, while Republican presidents such as Ronald Reagan and the two Bushes chose conservatives such as Antonin Scalia, Clarence Thomas, John Roberts and Samuel Alito.

We then saw in Chapter 2 that if a president is faced with the opportunity to fill a vacancy caused by the retirement or death of a justice of a different political philosophy to himself, he may be successful in actually changing the political balance of the Court. Thus in 1991, President George H. W. Bush, by replacing liberal justice Thurgood Marshall with conservative justice Clarence Thomas, was able to move the Court to the right. President George W. Bush managed a similar, though perhaps less dramatic, shift in 2006 when he replaced Sandra Day O'Connor with Samuel Alito.

The confirmation process

In Chapter 1, we discovered that the confirmation process of Supreme Court nominees in the Senate has evolved over the years. Initially, the Senate tended to take a rather laid-back approach to Court nominees — except on those occasions when they thought they warranted rejection. But unless there was any obvious controversy surrounding the nominee which might put his — and in those days it was always 'his' — nomination in jeopardy, the Senate generally confirmed nominees by voice vote, or on those rare occasions when a recorded vote was taken, it was virtually unanimous. But the last nominee to be confirmed by a voice vote was Abe Fortas back in 1965.

Even as recently as the 1980s and early 1990s, it was not unusual for the Senate to take a bipartisan approach to the confirmation of Supreme Court nominees. Hence, two current members of the Court were confirmed without any dissenting votes being cast at all — and one of those was Antonin Scalia, one of the most conservative members of the Court, who in 1986 was confirmed by a 98–0 vote. Even the then liberal lion of the Senate, the late Edward Kennedy of Massachusetts, voted for him. Indeed, it would have been 100–0 had not Republican senators Barry Goldwater of Arizona and Jake Garn of Utah been absent from the chamber that day. Liberal justice Ruth Bader Ginsburg attracted only three 'no' votes when she was confirmed by the Senate in 1993. Only conservative Republicans Robert Smith of New Hampshire, Don Nickles of Oklahoma and the legendry Jesse Helms of North Carolina voted 'no'.

But we saw in Chapter 1 that something of a turning point was reached in 1987 when the Democrat-controlled Senate rejected President Reagan's nomination of Robert Bork to the Supreme Court. That was followed by the unseemly matters which were raised in an attempt to discredit Clarence Thomas when he was nominated by President George H. W. Bush in 1991. Since then we have seen the trend for both political parties to use either support for or opposition to the nomination of Supreme Court justices as a way of mobilising their party's ideological base. Thus Democrats opposed the highly qualified Samuel Alito in 2006 and Republicans opposed the equally well-qualified Sonia Sotomayor in 2009.

The power of judicial review

Writing in *The Federalist Papers* at the time of the founding of the republic in the late eighteenth century, Alexander Hamilton famously described the judiciary as 'the least dangerous branch' of the federal government. But it was not long before all that changed. Just a few decades later Alexis de Tocqueville, a foreign observer of American politics, wrote: 'There is hardly a political question in the United States which does not sooner or later turn into a judicial one.' The change between these two observations must have something to do with the Supreme Court's acquisition of the power of judicial review in 1803.

The power of judicial review is the power of the Supreme Court to declare acts of Congress, or actions of the executive — or acts or actions of state governments — unconstitutional, and thereby null and void. This power puts the Court right in the midst of the political process of the United States, especially — but not exclusively — when it declares an act of Congress to be unconstitutional, thereby overturning the will of the elected majority in Congress. This is seen all the more so when the Court makes decisions in policy areas that are at the centre of political debate. Gone are the days when Justice Felix Frankfurter argued in *Colegrove* v *Green* (1946) that the Supreme Court ought not to hear cases relating to the apportionment of congressional districts — a highly political area — because 'courts ought not to enter this political thicket'.

By 1954, the Supreme Court was declaring in *Brown* v *the Board of Education of Topeka* that 'separate educational facilities are inherently unequal', and in so doing, declaring segregation to be unconstitutional. Here was something that had been a cornerstone of policy in the Deep South, as well as in such border and Midwestern states as Kansas, for generations, and it was being swept away not by the actions of elected officials, but by the nine-member, unelected Supreme Court.

In *Engel* v *Vitale* (1962), the Court declared prayers in public (i.e. state) schools to be unconstitutional. Ten years later, in *Furman* v *Georgia* (1972), the Court declared the death penalty as then imposed to be unconstitutional. The very next year, the Court handed down its landmark judgment in *Roe* v *Wade*, upholding a woman's right to an abortion by striking down a state law of Texas which prohibited this procedure as unconstitutional. Affirmative action programmes, internet pornography, flag burning, campaign finance laws, gun control, the rights of arrested persons — all these contentious political issues and more came under the scrutiny of the Supreme Court through its power of judicial review.

In these policy areas, we are looking at issues that divide the two major political parties: Democrats support abortion rights but oppose prayer in public schools; Republicans oppose abortion rights but support prayer in public schools. Democrats support affirmative action programmes and gun control legislation; Republicans oppose both. Republicans support the death penalty and stricter control of online pornography; Democrats oppose both. These issues have often taken centre stage in recent presidential election campaigns, as well as being central to many a House or Senate race. When the Supreme Court makes judgments in these kinds of contentious areas, it is bound to be seen as 'political'. What is more, it raises questions about what is the proper role of unelected judges in a modern democracy. Those who disagree with the Court in the landmark decisions it has reached in recent decades, criticise it as being an 'imperial judiciary', while the Court's supporters see the Court as playing its proper role of defending fundamental rights and liberties. How can these apparently contradictory views be reconciled?

The dilemma of the appropriate role of the Supreme Court is usually framed in terms of a battle between 'judicial activism' on the one side and 'judicial restraint' on the other. The trouble with this terminology is that it is not neutral. The term 'judicial activism' is all too often used pejoratively, usually indicating the disapproval of those who on any particular issue disagree with the Court's decision to strike down a federal or state law.

Judicial activism refers to the Supreme Court being willing to make significant changes in public policy by striking down federal or state laws, placing less importance than it might on precedent, and being less than deferential to the elected branches of government at both the federal and state level. Those who criticise the Court for being 'activist' also accuse its justices of 'legislating from the bench' or turning the Court into a 'super-legislature'.

Judicial restraint, on the other hand, refers to the Supreme Court seeing itself as merely the 'interpreter' of laws rather than the 'maker' of laws, placing great importance on precedence — what is often referred to in the Court's language as *stare decisis* (best translated as 'to stand by what has been already decided') — and being deferential to both Congress and the president as elected directly by the people.

Academics and commentators often appear to equate judicial activism with a liberal philosophy and judicial restraint with a conservative philosophy. But this is not necessarily accurate. An activist Court could be either liberal or conservative, depending on what laws it strikes down and what precedents it overturns. After all, were the Court, acting in an activist way, to overturn the principles of *Roe* v *Wade* and say that women in the USA do not have a constitutional right to an abortion, that would clearly be in line with conservative judicial philosophy. Equally, when the Court, acting in a restrained way, continues to agree with the Court's principles as announced in *Engel* v *Vitale* and other similar school prayer precedent-setting cases, it is clearly in line with a liberal judicial philosophy. Whatever the decision, whether to uphold this or overturn that, the decision is still viewed as having political implications and the Court is therefore viewed as being 'political'.

Bush v *Gore* (2000)

If ever the Court was viewed as a political institution, it was as a consequence of its decision in *Bush* v *Gore* in 2000, which effectively decided the result of that year's presidential election and handed the White House to George W. Bush and the Republicans. A brief setting of the scene is required.

By the end of election night, with the results in 49 of the 50 states declared, Bush had 246 Electoral College votes and Vice-President Al Gore, his Democrat opponent, had 267. Florida was still 'too close to call' and so its 25 Electoral College votes remained the decisive prize — whoever won Florida would win the presidency. Thus began a 35-day period of legal wrangling which would lead all the way to the United States Supreme Court.

By 18 November, after the ballots cast on Election Day had been counted mechanically, and then recounted mechanically, after some counties had completed some recounts by hand, and after the late-arriving overseas ballots had been added to the totals, Bush was ahead by a mere 930 votes out of almost 6 million that had been cast state-wide. The Florida secretary of state, Kathleen Harris, wanted to stop things there and certify Bush as the winner. But on 21 November, the Florida Supreme Court handed Gore an unexpected boost when it decided that Florida's final result should include all hand recounts. This was to prove a painfully slow business and would never be completed by the deadline, set for 5 p.m. on 26 November. It was at that hour that Kathleen Harris certified Bush as the winner of Florida's 25 Electoral College votes, to the cheers of Bush supporters outside the state Capitol in Tallahassee.

But Gore would not accept this verdict and said he would challenge it in the courts. After numerous toings-and-froings — too numerous to detail here — the case ended up on appeal by George W. Bush to the United States Supreme Court, where on 9 December the Court ordered all Florida court-ordered recounts to cease immediately 'pending further order of [this] Court'. In a 5–4 decision, Justice Antonin Scalia declared on that day for the majority:

> Though it is not customary for the Court to issue an opinion in connection with its grant of a stay, I believe a brief response is necessary…It suffices to say that the issuance of the stay suggests a majority of the Court, while not deciding the issues presented, believe that the petitioner [George W. Bush] has a substantial probability of success.

It sounded a bit like the King of Hearts in the trial scene in *Alice in Wonderland* — verdict first, trial later. Two days later — on Monday, 11 December — the Court did hear the case and it ruled the following day, by 7 votes to 2, that all the manual recounts ordered by the Florida Supreme Court violated the Equal Protection Clause of the Fourteenth Amendment. In a separate 5–4 ruling, the Court also decided that given the time constraints — the Electors in the Electoral College had to be named by midnight of 12 December, less than 2 hours after the Court issued its ruling — 'it is evident that any recount seeking to meet the 12 December date will be unconstitutional'. Writing for the majority, Justice Scalia remarked:

> Count first, and rule upon legality afterwards is not a recipe for producing election results that have the public acceptance democratic stability requires.

But in his dissenting opinion, Justice John Paul Stevens remarked that:

> Although we may never know with complete certainty the identity of the winner of this year's presidential election, the identity of the loser is perfectly clear: it is the nation's confidence in the judge [guarding] the rule of law.

Richard Posner, a judge of the United States Court of Appeals and a lecturer at the University of Chicago Law School, in his book *Breaking the Deadlock: The 2000 Election, the Constitution and the Courts* (Princeton University Press, 2001) later took Stevens and his dissenting colleagues to task for this remark.

> The four dissenting Justices did the Court no service by accusing the five-Justice majority of having impaired public confidence in the impartiality of the judiciary. Such an accusation, however heartfelt, is what is called fouling one's own nest. It also has an element of self-fulfilling prophecy: by telling the world that the decision would undermine public confidence in the courts, the dissenters made it more likely that it would indeed undermine public confidence in the courts…The majority decision, it is true, damaged the Court's prestige, at least in the short run; but it did not do so gratuitously — it averted a potential crisis.

It is somewhat naive to believe that ideology plays no role at all in the constitutional decisions made by the Supreme Court. But there is an important difference between what one might call political or judicial ideology and partisan politics. What was different about *Bush v Gore* was that it led many Democrats to accuse the five-member conservative majority of voting along party lines. The charge was amplified by pointing out that these conservative justices had voted against their usual ideological tendencies — for which they would normally have been congratulated by liberals! For in *Bush v Gore*, the conservative justices had argued for a wide interpretation of the Equal Protection Clause, something they would not normally do, and against leaving the matter up to the state government — their conventional position. But then, of course, the four dissenting liberal judges voted against their usual ideological tendencies as well — against a wide interpretation of the Fourteenth Amendment and for leaving things up to the state government. Judicial cross-dressing on this scale certainly does not improve the Court's standing with the public, especially when in effect deciding who will control the executive branch of government for the next 4 years. Arguments to suggest that the Supreme Court is a political institution were certainly much easier after *Bush v Gore*.

'Conservative' and 'liberal' justices

Yet another reason why we might regard the Supreme Court as a political institution is the political labels we attach to its members, in that we often refer to justices as being either 'conservative' or 'liberal', in much the same way as we might talk about members of Congress as conservatives or liberals. Some justices do not seem to fit either label, and they are often referred to as 'moderate' or 'swing' justices. We often use these ideological labels as a kind of shorthand.

By a conservative justice, we mean someone who tends to adhere to the principle of strict constructionism, who focuses on the text of the Constitution, who may even describe themselves as an originalist, who tends to distrust the power and scope of the federal government, preferring where possible to leave things to the states, and who was probably appointed by a Republican president. On the current Court, this would cover justices Antonin Scalia, Clarence Thomas, Samuel Alito and John Roberts.

By a liberal justice, we mean someone who tends to adhere to the principle of loose constructionism, who focuses on the context of the Constitution rather than just on the text, who may say that they believe in a living Constitution, who tends to think matters are better dealt with at the federal government level and is sceptical of leaving things to the individual states, and who was probably appointed by a Democratic president. On the current Court, this would cover justices Ruth Bader Ginsburg, Stephen Breyer, Sonia Sotomayor and Elena Kagan.

In the 'moderate' or 'swing' justice category, that leaves Anthony Kennedy, though he more closely fits into the conservative than the liberal grouping. Therefore, if one wanted to give an approximate left-to-right categorisation of the current Court, it would probably look something like this:

Ginsburg ⇒ Breyer ⇒ Sotomayor ⇒ Kagan ⇒ Kennedy ⇒ Roberts ⇒ Alito ⇒ Scalia ⇒ Thomas

All this, of course, needs to be taken with a considerable warning against over-categorisation and over-simplification, especially regarding the likely standing of Justice Kagan. Justices are complex people and the cases they are deciding are likewise complex. Very few justices can be entirely pigeonholed in this way. Nonetheless, there is absolutely no doubting that justices Stephen Breyer and Clarence Thomas come at things from a very different perspective, and this difference can be accurately designated in terms of political ideology.

Expansion and limitation of presidential power

As our definition of judicial review made very clear, this power does not refer only to acts of Congress, it refers also to actions of the president — or, for that matter, any member of the executive branch of government. Therefore, by its power of judicial review, the Supreme Court has at different times both expanded and limited presidential power. For just as the Court can say what the Constitution means when it comes to legislation, so it can say what the Constitution means when it comes to the powers of the president — what he may or may not constitutionally do.

Through most of its history the Supreme Court has expanded the grant of power to the president by offering broad interpretations of the precise wording of the Constitution when it comes to the president's powers in Article II. In the landmark decision of *Myers* v *United States* as far back as 1926, the Court granted the president the power to remove government officials without Congress's approval. In *Goldwater* v *Carter* (1979) the Court in effect upheld President Carter's termination of the 1954 Mutual Defence Treaty with Taiwan, and in the early 1980s the Court upheld various executive agreements made by presidents Carter and Reagan that followed the ending of the hostage crisis in Iran, which had occurred between November 1979 and January 1981.

But in recent decades, the Supreme Court has been much more likely to limit presidential power than to expand it. Back in 1952, in another landmark decision — *Youngstown Sheet and Tube Co.* v *Sawyer* — the Supreme Court stated that the ongoing Korean War did not excuse the seizure of American steel mills by the commerce secretary, Charles Sawyer, under orders from President Truman. Truman had ordered Sawyer to break a nationwide steel strike with federal troops, claiming that his commander-in-chief role in time of war allowed him to do this. The Court disagreed. It is worth noting that even one of Truman's own nominees to the Court, Tom Clark, joined the six-member majority in the decision, provoking the following outburst from President Truman:

> The damn fool from Texas that I first made Attorney General and then put on the Supreme Court! I don't know what got into me. He was no damn good as Attorney General, and on the Supreme Court, it doesn't seem possible but he's been even worse. He hasn't made one right decision that I can think of. And so when you ask me what my biggest mistake was, that's it — putting Tom Clark on the Supreme Court of the United States.

It's a cautionary tale for anyone tempted to think that Supreme Court appointees are presidential poodles.

In the Pentagon Papers case — *New York Times Co.* v *United States* — in 1971, the Court disagreed with President Nixon's claim of the principle of government control over classified documents when the Nixon White House tried to stop the *New York Times* from publishing classified material relating to the Vietnam War. Then in 1974, in *United States* v *Richard Nixon*, the Court disagreed with Nixon's claim of executive privilege, which he had used to refuse to hand over the so-called White House tapes relating to the Watergate affair. In an 8–0 decision, the Court declared that although executive privilege would apply in matters of defence and national security, it did not apply to the demand by Congress, the courts and the special prosecutor for the Watergate-related tapes. Even three of the four Nixon appointees on the Court — Harry Blackmun, Lewis Powell and Warren Burger — found against him. The other Nixon appointee, William Rehnquist, recused himself from the case because he had previously served in the Nixon administration as assistant attorney general. Up to this point, Nixon had denied unlimited access to the tape recordings of his Oval Office conversations. Only when the Supreme Court insisted he hand them over did the 'smoking gun' tape come to light which uncovered Nixon's lying and obstruction of justice. Sixteen days later, the president resigned — a fact which in itself underlines the political importance of the Supreme Court.

President Clinton found himself limited by the Court in what he could do on a number of fronts: executive privilege; presidential war making; lawyer–client privilege; and most famously, immunity from prosecution. In *William Jefferson*

Clinton v *Paula Corbin Jones* (1997), the Supreme Court upheld the appeal court's ruling that 'there is no immunity [from prosecution] for unofficial conduct' or from actions committed before the president entered office. It was a 9–0 decision, meaning that even Clinton's two appointees, Ruth Bader Ginsburg and Stephen Breyer, both found against him. It was the enquiries that followed from this decision by the Supreme Court which led to the disclosure of the president's relationship with White House intern Monica Lewinsky — another stark example of the political importance of Court decisions.

George W. Bush was also rebuffed on numerous occasions by decisions of the Supreme Court, mostly concerning national security and civil liberty issues stemming from the 'war on terror'. The Bush administration's policy for dealing with the Guantánamo Bay detainees received three defeats in 5 years at the hands of the Supreme Court. In *Rasul* v *Bush* (2004), the Court ruled

The detention centre at Guantánamo Bay

that the Guantánamo detainees did have access to the US federal courts to challenge their detention. The Bush administration had denied them this right, relying on a 1950 Court ruling that said war-time prisoners who were foreign nationals and who were held outside the United States were not eligible to have their cases heard in US courts. But Justice Sandra O'Connor disagreed. 'We have long since made it clear that a state of war is not a blank cheque for the president,' she stated.

Two years later, the Supreme Court was delivering another blow to the Bush administration in *Hamdan* v *Rumsfeld* (2006). In this decision, the Court clipped the wings of the president for employing military commissions to try the Guantánamo Bay detainees and for the use of warrantless wiretapping to get information about possible terrorist activity within the United States. Thus the Court questioned the broad assertion of presidential power which had become a hallmark of the Bush administration. By its decision, the Court was trying to redress the constitutional checks between the president and Congress by suggesting that only those tribunals specifically approved by Congress would pass muster with the Court. The military tribunals had received no such congressional approval: they were purely the invention of the Bush White House. This was certainly the line of argument pursued by Justice Stephen Breyer in his separate majority opinion:

> Where, as here, no emergency prevents consultation with Congress, judicial insistence upon that consultation does not weaken our Nation's ability to deal with danger. To the contrary, that insistence strengthens the Nation's ability to determine — through democratic means — how best to do so. The Constitution places its faith in those democratic means. Our Court today simply does the same.

Writing in the *Washington Post* immediately after the Court's judgment was announced ('A governing philosophy rebuffed', 30 June 2006), Bruce Fein, an official in the Reagan administration, stated that this ruling had restored the checks and balances within the federal government.

> What this decision says is, 'No, Mr President, you can be bound by treaties and statutes,' and if you need to have these changed, you can go to Congress and ask for their permission. The idea of a coronated president instead of an inaugurated president has been dealt a sharp rebuke.

Any institution of government that can, in effect, say 'No, Mr President' is potentially not only very powerful but political.

In 2008 came a third judgment of the Court to reverse the president's Guantánamo Bay policy. The judgment in *Boumediene* v *Bush* included a severe rebuke for the policies of the Bush administration, which had claimed that, as America was at war, the President had special powers to ensure the safety of the nation. 'The laws and Constitution are designed to survive, and remain in force, in extraordinary times,' wrote Justice Anthony Kennedy for the majority. 'To hold that the political branches may switch the Constitution on or off at will, would lead to a regime in which they, not this court, could say "what the law is,"' added Justice Kennedy, using language from the famous 1803 *Marbury* v *Madison* decision. President Bush was, needless to say, disappointed with the Court's decision. 'We'll abide by the Court's position,' said the President, 'but that doesn't mean I have to agree with it.'

And so we have seen how the Court has become a significant check on the power of the president. Of course, we should not expect the Supreme Court to be the sole or even the main accountability check on presidents. That role should be played by the democratically elected Congress. But although the Court may at times be criticised for 'entering the political thicket', it is surely to be encouraged that the Supreme Court continues to play a vital and an independent role in these kinds of case, one that is not intimidated by the other two branches of government. As Cronin and Genovese conclude (*The Paradoxes of the American Presidency*, 2004):

> Our system [of government] functions best when Congress, the president, and the Supreme Court each energetically promote its own independent vision of good government.

Therefore in this sense at least, the Supreme Court needs to continue to play a political role. But like its two competing institutions — Congress and the presidency — the Court is also subject to democratic control and accountability, including a certain degree of influence from public opinion.

Subject to democratic control and accountability

Finally, the Supreme Court, like other political institutions, is subject to democratic control and accountability. The Court is, first of all, subject to checks by Congress. We have already considered the Senate's power to confirm or reject appointments to the Court. It therefore has a hand in deciding who will, and who will not, be on the Court. Congress also has the power to decide the number of justices on the Court. Congress could increase the number of justices, thereby obliging the president to make new appointments and potentially altering the philosophical balance of the Court. Congress also has the power of impeachment and of trying cases of impeachment. Even the threat of impeachment can be effective, as it was in forcing the resignation of Justice Abe Fortas in 1969. Congress also has the power to initiate constitutional amendments that can in effect negate a decision of the Supreme Court.

Second, the Court is subject to checks by the president. By his power of nomination of justices to the Supreme Court, the president may be able to change the political and judicial philosophy of the Court. We have seen that this was the case when President George W. Bush nominated Samuel Alito to replace Sandra Day O'Connor in 2006. It is the president who, through the appointment power, in effect controls who sits on the Court. The president also decides whether or not to throw his political weight behind a decision of the Court. We have just seen President Bush's reaction to the *Boumediene* v *Bush* decision in 2008: 'We'll abide by the Court's position, but that doesn't mean I have to agree with it' — not exactly a ringing endorsement, and that can affect the public standing of the Court, especially if the president is himself popular (not something that was in Bush's favour in 2008). Following the Court's controversial First Amendment ruling in *Citizens United* v *Federal Election Commission* (2010), in which the Court struck down parts of the McCain–Feingold campaign finance reform legislation, President Obama was sharply critical of the Court's decision, calling it 'a green light to a new stampede of special interest money' in elections, and vowed to 'develop a forceful response' with congressional leaders to the ruling. The president claimed:

> This is a major victory for big oil, Wall Street banks, health insurance companies and other powerful interests that marshal their power every day in Washington to drown out the voices of everyday Americans.

Yet another important check on the Court — and one which once again highlights the Court as a political institution — is the check of public opinion. Of course, the Court is not subject to public opinion in the same way as the president and members of Congress. Justices are not subject to election. But that does not mean that the Court is entirely free from the effects of public approval or disapproval. If the Court makes decisions that fail to meet with broad public acceptance and approval, the consequences may be significant. There may be some reluctance by the general citizenry to obey such decisions, and as the Court has no means of its own to enforce compliance with its decisions, the Court would thereby be seen to lack both credibility and legitimacy, and that would of itself be serious. This was, after all, what lay behind Justice Stevens' remark in the dissenting judgment in *Bush* v *Gore* — that, in his view, 'the nation's confidence in the judge [guarding] the rule of law' had been damaged. Justice Souter, another of the dissenters in this case, was reported to be so upset by this decision that he contemplated resigning from the Court.

Table 5.1 shows that as the Court began a new term in September 2009, it enjoyed a higher rate of public approval than both Congress and President Obama. Figure 5.1 shows that Americans have held the Court in high esteem during recent years and, what is more, the data seem to disprove former Justice Stevens' comments concerning the possible effect of *Bush* v *Gore*.

Table 5.1 Public approval ratings of Congress, the president and the Supreme Court: September 2009

Branch of government	Approval rating
Supreme Court	61%
President Obama	54%
Congress	31%

Source: **www.gallup.com**

To illustrate the check of public opinion on the Court, take for example the issue of the Court's decisions concerning the Eighth Amendment regarding the death penalty. The Eighth Amendment forbids 'cruel and unusual punishments' and over the past few years the Court has had to decide on the constitutionality of both federal and state laws on a number of occasions. In *Atkins* v *Virginia* (2002) the Court decided that the execution of mentally retarded criminals

Figure 5.1 Public approval/disapproval of the Supreme Court: 2000–09

Gallup Poll
Do you approve or disapprove of the way the Supreme Court is handling its job?

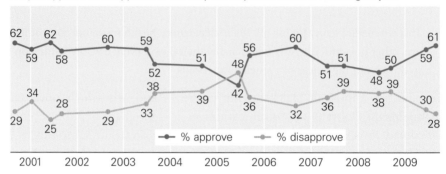

was unconstitutional. In *Roper* v *Simmons* (2005) the Court decided that it was unconstitutional to sentence anyone to death for a crime they committed when younger than 18. But in *Baze* v *Rees* (2008) the Court decided that lethal injection — the method used by the federal government and 35 states to execute criminals — did not constitute a 'cruel and unusual punishment'. So what the Court seemed to be saying was that it would allow capital punishment to continue (*Baze* v *Rees*) but would rule out certain uses of it (*Atkins* v *Virginia* and *Roper* v *Simmons*). Those conclusions are uncannily similar to where US public opinion is on the issue. Figure 5.2 shows that a majority of Americans (65%) still favour the death penalty, although by a smaller majority than was the case through the 1980s and 1990s.

Figure 5.2 Public support for/opposition to the death penalty in the United States: 1937–2009

Gallup Poll
Are you in favour of the death penalty for a person convicted of murder?

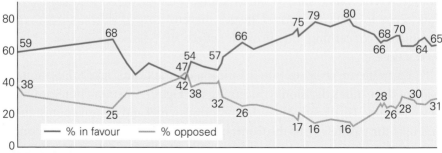

But the Gallup polling organisation asked another question at regular intervals during the past three decades or so: 'Do you feel that the death penalty acts as a deterrent to the commitment of murder, that it lowers the murder rate, or not?' In 1985, in answer to this question, 62% replied 'yes it does' while only 31% said 'no it doesn't'. By 2004, less than 20 years later, and at the time when the Court was handing down these decisions, the figures had pretty much switched round, with only 35% replying 'yes it does' and 62% saying 'no it doesn't'.

In 2002, the year in which the Supreme Court declared the execution of mentally retarded criminals unconstitutional, Gallup polling found that only 13% of Americans supported the execution of mentally retarded criminals, with 82% opposed. Public opinion on the execution of juveniles was much the same: only 26% supported whereas 69% opposed. So the Court's decisions were pretty much in line with public opinion. We are *not*, of course, suggesting that the Court merely looks up the latest polling on an issue that it is called upon to decide and votes accordingly. But we are making two valid points. First, had the Court *upheld* the execution of mentally retarded criminals and those who had committed their crimes when juveniles, it would have been way out of step with the prevailing opinion of the day, and that would have caused the Court significant problems in terms of public acceptance and credibility. The same would have been true had the Court in 2008, by declaring lethal injection unconstitutional, made the death penalty virtually inoperable in the United States. Second, the Court often exhibits a characteristic of other political bodies of treading a middle path on controversial matters affecting American society. We could equally have argued this by looking at the Court's ruling on abortion rights during the same period — unwilling to say either that women have an unlimited right to an abortion or that they have no such rights at all, pretty much where the majority of Americans stand on the issue.

Conclusion

The Supreme Court is, of course, first and foremost a judicial institution. But its members are appointed by politicians and confirmed by politicians. It is called upon to make decisions on matters that are at the forefront of political debate in the United States. It has sometimes expanded, but more recently limited, the power of the president; indeed, it might even have been said to have forced a president from office in 1974, and elected a president to office in 2000. Like other political institutions, it is subject to checks and balances. Justices of the Supreme Court do not operate in a political vacuum; they operate in the real world, beset by political controversies that they are often called upon to arbitrate. They are not politicians, but neither are they political eunuchs. They do not make decisions based upon public opinion polling, but in making their decisions they need to have some degree of confidence that their decisions will be accepted as reasonable and legitimate. In that sense, it is true to say that the United States Supreme Court is a judicial body with significant political overtones.

Task 5.1

Source A is adapted from an article by Robert Barnes in the *Washington Post* on 22 January 2010, immediately following the Supreme Court's decision in *Citizens United* v *Federal Election Commission*, in which the Court declared parts of the McCain–Feingold campaign reform act unconstitutional. This was a landmark First Amendment case, and because it concerned the issue of campaign finance, it had clear political overtones. Read Source A and then answer the questions that follow.

Source A

High Court shows it might be willing to act boldly

The Roberts Court ended its term last summer avoiding a constitutional showdown with Congress over the Voting Rights Act. But its first major decision of the current term might signal a new willing-ness to act boldly. Chief Justice John Roberts and his conservative colleagues delivered a seismic jolt on Thursday. They overturned two of the Court's past decisions — including one made as recently as 6 years ago — to upend federal legislation that says corporations may not use their profits to support or oppose candidates and to declare unconstitutional a large portion of the McCain–Feingold campaign finance reform act passed in 2002.

The Court's future (Chief Justice Roberts and Associate Justice Alito were key to the decision) and its past (89-year-old John Paul Stevens led his liberal colleagues in dissent) were on vivid display at the Court's special session to deliver all 176 pages of *Citizens United* v *Federal Election Commission*.

Although the majority's ode to the First Amendment was announced by Justice Anthony Kennedy, it would not have been possible without Roberts and Alito, President George W. Bush's nominees to the Court. Roberts has shown himself more willing than his mentor and predecessor, William Rehnquist, to question the Court's past decisions. Alito's replacement of Justice Sandra Day O'Connor has tipped the Court's balance from supportive of congressional efforts to reduce the influence of special interests to suspicious of how the restrictions curtail free speech. Roberts, Alito and Kennedy were joined in their majority opinion by fellow conservative justices Scalia and Thomas.

The dissent was read hesitantly by Stevens, the Court's longest-serving justice. He wrote of his conservative colleagues' 'agenda' and said they had transformed a simple case about whether a conservative group's movie about Hillary Rodham Clinton [shown during her 2008 presidential primary campaign] violated the McCain–Feingold Act into a major constitutional argument. 'Essentially, five justices were unhappy with the limited nature of the case before us, so they changed the case to give themselves an opportunity to change the law.'

Task 5.1 (Continued)

The battle over restricting corporate and union spending in political campaigns does not break along ideological lines: the American Civil Liberties Union and the National Rifle Association both supported Citizens United, the conservative group who brought the case. But the reaction to the Court's decision followed mostly partisan lines. And the Court's familiar ideological split may have reinforced the image the Court finds most distasteful — that its decisions are political as well.

(a) Explain the author's reference to the decision in this case being a 'seismic jolt'.

(b) How did the Court split in this decision: which justices were on which side of the decision?

(c) Explain Justice Stevens' accusation in the fourth paragraph.

(d) What evidence is given that, in terms of groups supporting Citizens United, this battle 'does not break along ideological lines'?

(e) Why do you think the author suggests (i) that this decision would be seen as political, and (ii) that the Court finds this 'most distasteful'?

Guidance

(a) You may need to look up the word 'seismic' in a dictionary: once you know the meaning of that word, you should be able to understand what the author means.

(b) This is quite straightforward: think 'conservatives' and 'liberals' plus one 'swing justice'.

(c) Try to get the phrase 'judicial activism' into your answer — and notice that this accusation is being levelled at conservative judges.

(d) You need to find out, if you do not know already, the ideological bent of the ACLU and the NRA.

(e) (i) Looking back at the comments made by President Obama following the announcement of this decision will certainly give you a clue.

(ii) Think about whether Supreme Court justices think of themselves as 'politicians' and why attaching the adjective 'political' to their decisions would displease them.

Task 5.2

Source B (page 90) gives some statistics on the Supreme Court over a 10-year period, from 2000 to 2010. Study the data and then answer the questions that follow.

(a) The percentage of Supreme Court cases which, in any given term, is decided by a 5–4 split varies from just 13% in 2005–06 up to 33% in 2006–07. Why might it be better when this percentage is lower rather than higher?

(b) What is significant about the data on the justice(s) most in the majority in 5–4 decisions between 2000/2001 and 2004/05, and between 2005/06 and 2009/10?

(c) Which justice has most frequently been in the minority in 5–4 decisions over this 10-year period? What does that tell us about the ideological centre of the Court?

Source B

Selected statistics on the Supreme Court: 2000–10

Term:	2000–01	2001–02	2002–03	2003–04	2004–05	2005–06	2006–07	2007–08	2008–09	2009–10
Number of decisions	79	76	73	73	74	69	68	67	74	86
% which were 5–4 decisions	30%	26%	19%	27%	30%	13%	33%	17%	31%	19%
Justice(s) most in majority in 5–4 decisions	O'Connor Kennedy	O'Connor	O'Connor	O'Connor	O'Connor Kennedy Scalia Thomas Souter	Kennedy	Kennedy	Kennedy Thomas	Kennedy	Kennedy Thomas Scalia
Justice(s) most in minority in 5–4 decisions	Breyer Stevens	Ginsburg	Breyer Ginsburg Stevens	Breyer Ginsburg Souter	Rehnquist Stevens	Breyer	Stevens	Breyer	Breyer	Ginsburg
% of which conservatives won 5–4 decisions	54%	38%	40%	48%	21%	55%	54%	33%	48%	50%
% of which liberals won 5–4 decisions	31%	29%	33%	33%	33%	36%	25%	33%	22%	19%
Two justices most in agreement	Breyer Ginsburg	Souter Ginsburg	Scalia Thomas	Souter Ginsburg	Souter Ginsburg	Roberts Alito	Roberts Alito	Roberts Scalia	Roberts Alito	Ginsburg Sotomayor
Two justices most in disagreement	Scalia Stevens	Scalia Ginsburg	Thomas Breyer	Scalia Stevens	Thomas Stevens	Alito Stevens	Thomas Stevens	Thomas Stevens	Thomas Stevens	Thomas Stevens
Justice(s) most in the majority	O'Connor	O'Connor Rehnquist	O'Connor	O'Connor	Breyer	Roberts	Kennedy	Roberts	Kennedy	Roberts Kennedy
Justice(s) most in the minority	Stevens	Stevens	Thomas	Scalia	Stevens	Stevens	Stevens	Thomas	Stevens	Stevens

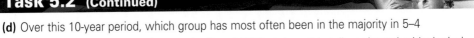

Task 5.2 (Continued)

(d) Over this 10-year period, which group has most often been in the majority in 5–4 decisions — the conservatives or the liberals? What does this tell us about the ideological centre of the Court?

(e) What do the data on the two justices most in agreement tell us about the two George W. Bush appointees to the Court?

(f) To what extent do the data on the two justices most in disagreement support the ideological categorisation of the Court given earlier in the chapter?

(g) What conclusions do you draw from the bottom two rows of Source B about the ideological centre of the Court during this period?

Guidance

(a) You need to consider what a 5–4 decision implies about the differing views of the justices, and why decisions made with more justices being in agreement might carry more weight.

(b) Comment on who dominates the list in the first period and then in the second period. Also think how this ties in with the liberal $\Rightarrow$ conservative categorisation:

Stevens $\Rightarrow$ Ginsburg $\Rightarrow$ Breyer $\Rightarrow$ Sotomayor $\Rightarrow$ Kennedy $\Rightarrow$ Roberts $\Rightarrow$ Alito $\Rightarrow$ Scalia $\Rightarrow$ Thomas

(c) Look at where this justice appears on the categorisation above.

(d) This is quite a straightforward question.

(e) Note their level of agreement, and also the 2007–08 column. What does this tell you about Alito?

(f) Match the data in this row with the categorisation above.

(g) See where those most often in the majority and in the minority sit on the ideological spectrum above: that will help you draw conclusions about the ideological centre of the Court during this period.

6 Should Supreme Court justices still be appointed for life?

An early twentieth-century Nebraska senator, George W. Norris, once remarked: 'The people can change Congress, but only God can change the Supreme Court!' What Senator Norris was alluding to was the fact that, whereas the people can vote members of Congress out of office, there is no way — short of impeachment, trial and conviction — that members of the Supreme Court can be removed against their will, other than by death; hence Senator Norris's reference to God. Supreme Court justices enjoy life tenure. They may choose to retire, as did justices David Souter in 2009 and John Paul Stevens in 2010. Otherwise they remain in office until they die — as did Chief Justice William Rehnquist, who served for just short of 34 years on the Court, from 1971 until his death in 2005.

But should Supreme Court justices still be appointed for life? We need to see why the Founding Fathers decided to write this into the Constitution. What are the pros and cons of life tenure? Then we shall see what has happened during the 220 or so years of Supreme Court history. How have the majority of justices left the Court — by death, resignation or retirement? Why has the impeachment process not been used to remove any justices of the Supreme Court? Should term limits be introduced for Supreme Court justices, and what about a mandatory retirement age? And, finally — and most radically — should the justices be elected, as judges are in many of the state judiciaries?

The Founding Fathers' reasoning

Article III of the Constitution states that Supreme Court justices 'shall hold their Offices during good Behaviour'. This delightfully vague provision raises two issues: life tenure and impeachment. If justices are to hold office 'during good behaviour' — whatever that means — then clearly the only way they could be forced from office is because of 'bad behaviour'. Or to put it another way, provided justices continued to exhibit 'good behaviour' they could remain in office for as long as they wished. Alexander Hamilton, one of the notable framers, saw justices' life tenure as a most important strength of the new Constitution. In Hamilton's view, the fact that the justices would hold office for life was a guarantee of judicial independence.

Hamilton addressed this issue in number 78 of *The Federalist* and came up with four reasons why life tenure was desirable. First, argued Hamilton, it was the pattern most popularly used in the various states which were to make up the Union, as well as in Great Britain. Second, Hamilton saw life tenure as an important requirement in order to guarantee limited, democratic government. As Hamilton stated:

> The standard of good behavior for the continuance in office of the judicial magistracy, is certainly one of the most valuable of the modern improvements in the practice of government. In a monarchy it is an excellent barrier to the despotism of the prince; in a republic it is a no less excellent barrier to the encroachments and oppressions of the representative body. And it is the best expedient which can be devised in any government, to secure a steady, upright, and impartial administration of the laws.

On this point, Hamilton was even more specific. It is worthy of note that at the birth of the nation, the framers were just as concerned about the possibility of an over-powerful Congress as they were about an over-powerful president.

> If, then, the courts of justice are to be considered as the bulwarks of a limited Constitution against legislative encroachments, this consideration will afford a strong argument for the permanent tenure of judicial offices, since nothing will contribute so much as this to that independent spirit in the judges which must be essential to the faithful performance of so arduous a duty.

Hamilton therefore had a third reason why he regarded life tenure as important — it was a critical ingredient in guaranteeing the independence of the judiciary, what Hamilton calls here 'that independent spirit in the judges'.

Finally, Hamilton believed that only if the justices had life tenure would the right people be prepared to give up their current professions and commit themselves to the service of the Court. Hamilton argued that, as the issues the justices would be called upon to decide were likely to be complex, and the body of law they would have to master so vast, life tenure was critical to the good performance of their office. And so it was that for these reasons, the Founding Fathers incorporated life tenure for the justices of the Supreme Court — indeed, for all federal judges — into the new Constitution.

The changing scene

But Alexander Hamilton and his fellow framers had little reason to ponder the possibility that one day most Supreme Court justices would serve longer than your average medieval monarch. Of the first ten justices of the Supreme Court, only two lived to the age of 70, and their average length of service was under 8 years. Of the last ten justices to leave the Supreme Court, all have lived to the age of 70 — indeed, three reached their nineties — and their average length of service was just under 25 years. As Stuart Taylor concluded in an article in *The Atlantic* magazine ('Life Tenure Is Too Long For Supreme Court Justices', 28 June 2005): 'Thus have modern medicine — and modern justices' fondness for their power and glory — transformed the meaning of life tenure.'

Table 6.1 Justices leaving the Supreme Court: 1881–1910

Justice	Date of leaving Court	Reason	Years of Court service	Age on leaving Court	Age at death
Noah Swayne	1881	Retired	19	76	79
Nathan Clifford	1881	Died	23	77	77
Ward Hunt	1882	Disabled	9	72	76
William Woods	1887	Died	6	63	63
Morrison Waite	1888	Died	14	71	71
Stanley Matthews	1889	Died	7	65	65
Samuel Miller	1890	Died	28	74	74
Joseph Bradley	1892	Died	21	78	78
Lucius Lamar	1893	Died	5	67	67
Samuel Blatchford	1893	Died	11	73	73
Howell Jackson	1895	Died	2	73	73
Stephen Field	1897	Retired	34	81	82
Horace Gray	1902	Died	20	74	74
George Shiras	1903	Retired	10	71	92
Henry Brown	1906	Retired	15	70	77
Rufus Peckham	1909	Died	13	70	70
Melville Fuller	1910	Died	22	77	77
David Brewer	1910	Died	20	72	72
William Moody	1910	Retired	4	56	63
Average	–	–	**14.9 years**	**71.6 years**	**73.8 years**

| | Table 6.2 | Justices leaving the Supreme Court: 1981–2010 | | | | |

Justice	Date of leaving Court	Reason	Years of Court service	Age on leaving Court	Age at death
Potter Stewart	1981	Retired	22	66	70
Warren Burger	1986	Retired	17	79	87
Lewis Powell	1987	Retired	16	79	90
William Brennan	1990	Retired	33	84	91
Thurgood Marshall	1991	Retired	24	83	84
Byron White	1993	Retired	31	76	84
Harry Blackmun	1994	Retired	24	85	90
William Rehnquist	2005	Died	34	80	80
Sandra Day O'Connor	2006	Retired	24	75	*
David Souter	2009	Retired	19	69	*
John Paul Stevens	2010	Retired	34	90	*
Average	–	–	**25.2 years**	**78.7 years**	**84.5 years**

*still alive at time of writing

If one compares the departures from the Court during 1981–2010 with what was happening exactly a century earlier, one sees a very stark contrast (see Tables 6.1 and 6.2). Between 1981 and 2010, 11 justices left the Court — only 1 (9%) by death. But between 1881 and 1910, 19 justices left the Court, of whom 13 (68%) died in office. Indeed, 8 justices died in one 8-year period alone, between 1887 and 1895. Or look at it this way: when the Court resumed for its new term in October 1887, 7 of its 9 members would be dead within the next 10 years, and an eighth would last only 5 years longer!

Between these two periods, the average years of service rose significantly from 15 years (1881–1910) to 25 years (1981–2010). The age at which justices died also rose from 74 (1881–1910) to 84 (1981–2010). The figure that changed least was the average age at which justices left the Court, which rose from 71 to 78. This was because although justices now serve longer, they tend to be appointed younger. Of the 11 justices who left the Court between 1981 and 2010, 3 — Potter Stewart, Bryon White and William Rehnquist — had been appointed to the Court while still in their forties. Only 2 of the 19 justices appointed in the earlier period were under 50.

The significant change in life expectancy since the days of the Founding Fathers has had a dramatic effect on the Court as a result of the life tenure which justices enjoy. In the first 100 years of the Court (1789–1889), 27 justices died in office;

Chapter 6

Table 6.3 Life expectancy at birth: 1850–2004

Calendar period	White males	White females	All other males	All other females
1850	38.3	40.5	–	–
1890	42.5	44.5	–	–
1900-02	48.2	51.1	32.5	35.0
1909-11	50.2	53.6	34.1	37.7
1919-21	56.3	58.5	47.1	46.9
1929-31	59.1	62.7	47.6	49.5
1939-41	62.8	67.3	52.3	55.5
1949-51	66.3	72.0	58.9	62.7
1959-61	67.6	74.2	61.5	66.4
1969-71	67.9	75.5	61.0	69.1
1979-81	70.8	78.2	65.6	74.0
1990	72.7	79.4	67.0	75.2
2000	74.8	80.0	68.3	75.0
2004	75.7	80.8	69.8	76.5

during the second 100 years (1889–1989), 21 justices died in office. But when Rehnquist died in September 2005, he was the first justice of the Supreme Court to die in office for over 50 years. This cursory glance at the statistics would suggest that it has therefore become less fashionable, maybe less acceptable, to continue in office on the Supreme Court until one's death. Table 6.3 shows how life expectancy has increased in the USA even in the period since 1850. The life expectancy of white males, for example, has doubled during the past 150 years.

Justice John Paul Stevens in 2006, aged 86

©Danita Delimont/Alamy

All these statistics, therefore, suggest that justices are both living longer and staying longer on the Court. The scene has changed to an extent which would have been unimaginable to the Founding Fathers. This is the conclusion of Roger Cramton and Paul Carrington in their detailed study of the Supreme Court, *Reforming the Court: Term Limits for Supreme Court Justices* (Carolina Academic Press, 2006). In their view:

> These historical trends represent nothing short of a revolution in the practical meaning of the Constitution's grant of life tenure to Supreme Court justices.

> The Framers gave life tenure in an era when the average American could expect
> to live to only 35 years of age.

Cramton and Carrington see three further problems caused by the life tenure of justices. First, vacancies occur far less frequently. There were no vacancies on the Court between November 1975 and July 1981, between July 1981 and September 1986, and between August 1994 and September 2005. Because of the first of those periods, Jimmy Carter became the only president to serve a complete term in office and make no appointments to the Court. Neither Bill Clinton's second term (1997–2001) nor George W. Bush's first term (2001–05) saw any Court vacancies.

This, according to these two academics, leads to a second problem — that when a vacancy does occur, it takes on an intensity and importance which never used to be the case. In other words, Cramton and Carrington see life tenure as a contributory cause to some of those problems regarding the nomination and confirmation process that we discussed in Chapter 1.

Thirdly, Cramton and Carrington believe that, as many justices now serve so long on the Court, they are in danger of becoming out-of-touch and out-of-date. Some clearly keep going well beyond their sell-by date. William Douglas, who set the record for Supreme Court tenure — 37 years between 1939 and 1975 — barely functioned during his last 10 months, after a debilitating stroke in 1975. Colleagues even came to an informal agreement to nullify any decision in which Justice Douglas cast the deciding vote. Thurgood Marshall (1967–91) was a shadow of his former self when he eventually retired, aged 83, even admitting on his last day in Court: 'I'm getting old and falling apart.' Chief Justice William Rehnquist was desperately ill with cancer during much of his final year in office, appearing frail and almost voiceless as he officiated at the second George W. Bush inauguration less than 9 months before he died in office. In January 2010, the *Washington Post*, reporting the Court's judgment in *Citizens United* v *FEC*, noted that 89-year-old Justice John Paul Stevens 'read hesitantly' from his dissenting opinion and 'stumbled uncharacteristically' during his 20-minute address from the bench. According to Professor Larry Sabato of the University of Virginia:

> The insularity of lifetime tenure, combined with the appointments of relatively young attorneys who give long service on the bench, produces senior judges representing the views of past generations better than views of the current day.

So we have discovered thus far the reasons for the framers granting justices life tenure, but have found that, given increased longevity, the situation has changed significantly from the latter days of the eighteenth century and this has brought about some unforeseen negatives to the practice of life tenure. This then leads us to the question: what, if anything, should be done about it?

Impeachment — the dog that barked only once

So far we have considered the rate at which justices have left the Court by resignation, retirement or death. But there is, of course, a fourth way by which justices can leave the Supreme Court and it is directly related to the issue of life tenure. We have already seen that Article III of the Constitution states that Supreme Court justices 'shall hold their Offices during good Behaviour.' This not only grants life tenure but also raises the possibility of impeachment, trial, conviction and removal from office. Supreme Court justices may be impeached by the House of Representatives and then tried by the Senate; if found guilty by the Senate by a two-thirds majority, they would be removed from office.

But in its history of over 220 years, only one Supreme Court justice has ever been impeached — Justice Samuel Chase in 1804. This impeachment was so blatantly one of political motivation that, according to most commentators, it permanently discredited the use of impeachment to intimidate justices whose political views arouse congressional or presidential hostility. Chase was impeached on eight counts and on not one of them did the Senate get near to the required two-thirds majority for conviction and removal from office.

Impeachment threats were aimed at two Supreme Court justices in the late 1960s — Abe Fortas and William Douglas. Fortas was a crony of President Lyndon Johnson, who had nominated him to the Court in 1965. Three years later, Chief Justice Earl Warren informed President Johnson of his intention to retire. Johnson now came up with a plan whereby Fortas would be elevated to the chief justiceship and another Johnson crony, Homer Thornberry, would be appointed to the Court as an associate justice. The plan backfired badly. Fortas, who had been confirmed by the Senate as an associate justice just 3 years earlier by a voice vote, had to undergo further scrutiny in order to be confirmed as chief justice. It was during this second set of Judiciary Committee hearings that interest came to focus on a $15,000 fee that Fortas had received from American University for participating in a lecture series. Fortas's nomination became the subject of a Republican-led filibuster on the Senate floor and it soon became clear that the nomination was a hopeless cause. Fortas wrote to the president asking for his name to be withdrawn — a request to which Johnson reluctantly agreed. With the presidential election less than a month away, Johnson had lost his opportunity to make the Court appointments. By the following year, Fortas was facing the possibility of impeachment and he resigned from the Court in May 1969. Republican president Richard Nixon got to replace both Warren as Chief Justice and Fortas as an associate justice.

Then in April 1970, moves began to impeach another associate justice, William O. Douglas. By this time, the 71-year-old Douglas had already served 31 years on the Court since his appointment by FDR. But it was not his longevity or long service that were the problems so much as his long line of former wives. Douglas married four times — including three times in 11 years, between 1954 and 1965. His third and fourth wives were law students in their early twenties! Douglas was virtually bankrupted by the financial settlements with his first three wives and had to rely on the income from publishing and lectures to make ends meet. By 1970, some members of the House of Representatives wanted to investigate Douglas's financial links to a dodgy casino owner and hotel proprietor in Las Vegas. The move was spearheaded by Congressman Gerald Ford of Michigan, who in just 4 years would become vice-president and then president of the United States. Ford takes up the story in his autobiography, *A Time to Heal* (Harper and Row, 1979):

> Most people believe that federal judges are appointed for life. Actually, the Constitution says that they shall serve only during periods of 'good behavior'. Convinced that Douglas's behavior had failed that test, his opponents in the House wanted to launch impeachment proceedings against him. On the evening of April 15, 1970, I made a speech on the floor [of the House] in which I laid out the information that our probe had uncovered. I didn't call for Douglas's impeachment. Instead, I asked the House to appoint a select committee that would have 90 days to determine whether or not grounds for impeachment existed.

But that never happened. The matter was referred to the House Judiciary Committee, which was stacked with liberal Democrats who supported Douglas, and the matter died. In Ford's view, a disreputable justice had been let off the hook.

Since 1789, the House of Representatives has impeached 18 federal officials — 1 senator, 1 cabinet officer, 2 presidents and 14 members of the federal judiciary. Twelve of those 14 federal judges, however, were trial court judges — most recently Judge Samuel Kent in June 2009. One other was a circuit court (appellate) judge, and just one was a justice of the Supreme Court. Critics of the life tenure enjoyed by Supreme Court justices would suggest that there has been more than one rotten apple in the barrel of — thus far — 111 Supreme Court justices. The failure of the Congress, therefore, to take its impeachment powers seriously may be regarded as another weakness in the life tenure argument.

So far, the argument for life tenure has been seen to have both pros and cons. But if the cons are to be taken seriously, then some alternatives must be proposed: if not life tenure, then what? Three proposals deserve careful analysis: term limits; a mandatory retirement age; and election.

A fixed, non-renewable term for justices?

Putting some kind of limit on the tenure of Supreme Court justices should not be regarded as particularly radical. After all, only one state — Rhode Island — gives to its state Supreme Court justices the security of life tenure enjoyed by all federal judges, and even in Rhode Island, Supreme Court justices can be recalled by a majority vote of the state legislature. All the other 49 states impose some kind of limit on the tenure of the justices on their highest court. According to Cramton and Carrington:

> The nearly unanimous consensus against life tenure for state judges, both on the highest courts and on intermediate appellate courts, is telling, and it provides further evidence of the undesirability of maintaining a system of life tenure in the present day.

They also point out that the legal system upon which the Founding Fathers based the US system — that in Great Britain — has eliminated the guarantee of life tenure for its judges. Currently in the UK, all judges appointed to office after 31 March 1995 must retire at 70, while those appointed on or before then must retire at 75, and this applies to justices of the new UK Supreme Court.

In *Reforming the Court: Term Limits for Supreme Court Justices*, Cramton and Carrington recommend a constitutional amendment imposing an 18-year, staggered term limit for Supreme Court justices. Their proposal would be to stagger the terms so that a vacancy would be created on the Court every 2 years during the first and third years of a president's 4-year term. Justices' terms would end on the last day of the Court's term in June in any given year and the new justice's term would begin on the first day of the Court's new term the following October, thereby allowing time for confirmation hearings to take place. The amendment would not apply to the appointments made by the president at the time of its passage, beginning with his successor, and neither would it apply retrospectively to the justices on the Court at the time of passage. They would be permitted to enjoy life tenure. If a justice appointed for a fixed term died, resigned or retired before the completion of their 18-year term, an interim justice would be appointed by the incumbent president, subject to the usual checks of Senate confirmation. This justice, however, would then be ineligible for appointment to a full 18-year term on the Court.

The authors see this proposal as having a number of advantages. First, it would reverse the increase in the average tenure of justices on the Supreme Court. Between 1789 and 1970, justices served an average of 14.9 years on the Court, but in the period since 1970 this has increased to over 26 years. Similarly, the average age at which justices retired or died between 1789 and 1970 was 68, while in the period since 1970 this has increased to 80. A fixed 18-year term would reverse both these trends and put them more into line with what the Founding Fathers might have envisaged.

Second, it would even up the intervals at which vacancies occur. All one-term presidents would make two appointments to the Court and two-term presidents would appoint four justices. There would no longer be periods such as between 1994 and 2005 when there were no appointments at all. Equally, it would stop the occurrence of what one might call 'appointment hot spots' — a rush of appointments during a short period of time. FDR appointed five justices in a 2½-year period between August 1937 and January 1940; Nixon appointed three justices in a 1½-year period between June 1970 and January 1972. With Supreme Court nominations coming at regular intervals, the advocates of this plan also suggest that it would take some of the heat out of the confirmation process.

A third benefit according to the plan's supporters is that it would stop justices timing their retirement in order to try to affect the likely judicial philosophy of their replacement. One could not have envisaged the aged John Paul Stevens retiring during George W. Bush's presidency knowing that he would probably have been replaced by a much more conservative justice. Cramton and Carrington argue:

> By making vacancies a regular occurrence, and by limiting the stakes of each confirmation to an eighteen-year term rather than the thirty-year period that has recently prevailed for some justices, our proposal should reduce the intensity of partisan warfare in the confirmation process. Under the current system of life tenure, the uncertainty over when the next vacancy on the Supreme Court might arise, as well as the possibility that any given nominee could serve for up to four decades on the Court, means the political pressures on the president and the Senate in filling any Supreme Court vacancy are tremendous. Our proposed amendment, by eliminating nearly all of the uncertainty over the timing of vacancies and by reducing the stakes associated with each appointment, promises to reduce the intensity of the political fights over confirmation.

So what are the potential negatives of this proposal? First, critics of the term-limit proposal suggest that it would impair the judicial independence of the Court. As we have already seen, the Founding Fathers wrote life tenure into the Constitution in order to guarantee the independence of the Court. Alexander Hamilton argued that life tenure would secure the freedom of a judge from both Congress and the president, as well as from public opinion, ensuring that judges can objectively interpret the Constitution without risk of political reprisal. Impinging upon life tenure, it is argued, could jeopardise this independence. However, as this specific proposal is one of a fixed and non-renewable term, it could be argued that judicial independence would still be sufficiently guaranteed.

Second, it is argued that, were a political party to win, for example, three or more consecutive presidential elections, the party could in effect 'capture the Court'. To take a concrete example, had this proposal been in effect in the 1980s when the Republicans won three consecutive elections — with Ronald Reagan in 1980 and 1984, followed by George H. W. Bush in 1988 — those three presidents would have appointed six of the nine members of the Court. However, this argument too may be somewhat exaggerated. After all, under life tenure presidents Reagan and Bush between them appointed five Supreme Court justices during these 12 years of Republican control — O'Connor, Scalia, Kennedy, Souter and Thomas.

Third, it is argued that the introduction of a fixed term for Supreme Court justices would encourage justices to become more activist by, as Cramton and Carrington put it, 'endangering the virtue of patience that life tenure affords' to justices of the Supreme Court. Responding to a Senate Judiciary Committee questionnaire during his confirmation hearings in 1988, Justice Anthony Kennedy had this to say in defence of federal judges' life tenure:

> Life tenure is in part a constitutional mandate to the federal judiciary to proceed with caution, to avoid reaching issues not necessary to the resolution of the case at hand, and to defer to the political process.

Cramton and Carrington raise a further possible negative of the fixed-term proposal in stating:

> Justices in their final years in office might face a final period incentive to go out with a splash, knowing that in a short time they might no longer have to work with and live with their current Supreme Court colleagues.

Alternatively, it is also possible that the reverse may occur — that justices in their final 2 years, just before their forced retirement, might become 'lame duck' justices whose opinions would carry less weight than those of their more recently appointed colleagues — a sort of judicial equivalent to a lame duck president in the final 2 years of his second term.

A fifth possible negative to this proposal is that it would erode the prestige of the Court by making the term-limited positions less attractive than those offered appointment. It might also have the unintended and unfortunate side-effect of justices being appointed later in their judicial careers, not wanting to be thrown on the scrapheap in their early sixties. Had this proposal been in place when the 43-year-old Clarence Thomas was appointed to the Court in 1991, he would have been forced to retire in 2009 at the age of only 61. Were this proposal not extended to other federal judges, Justice Thomas's former federal appeal court colleagues would still be able to look forward to 10, maybe 20 or more, years of judicial service when reaching such an age. This would surely encourage justices to join the Court at an older age if at all possible.

A mandatory retirement age for justices?

Most of these negatives would also apply to another proposal — to replace life tenure with a mandatory retirement age. As we have already noted, many states already impose a mandatory retirement age on their state court judges (see Figure 6.1). At the end of 2011, Chief Justice Gerry Alexander of the state

Figure 6.1　Retirement ages for state judges

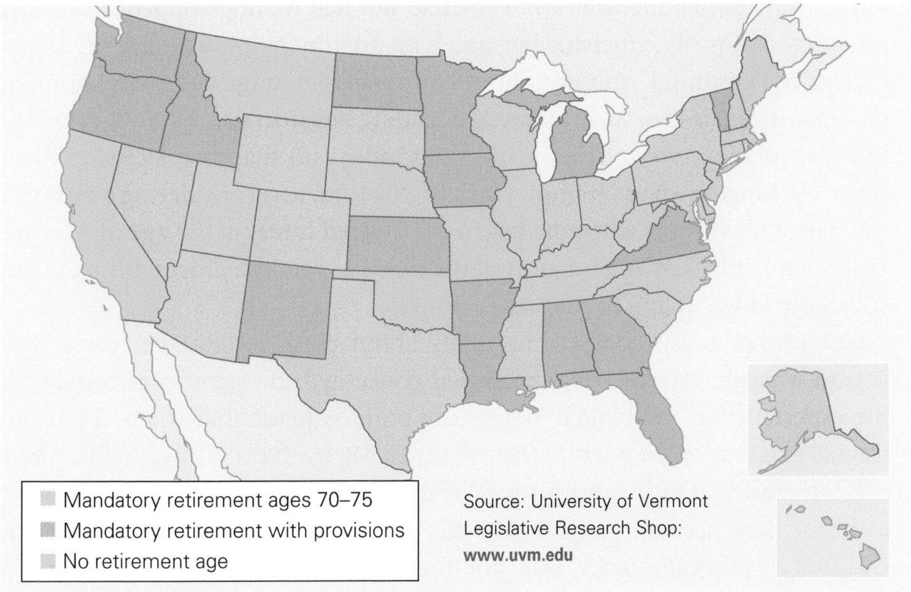

- Mandatory retirement ages 70–75
- Mandatory retirement with provisions
- No retirement age

Source: University of Vermont Legislative Research Shop: www.uvm.edu

of Washington will be forced to step down from the state's highest court, having reached the age of 75. 'As I sit here looking out through these eyes, I feel the same as I did when I became a judge. I think I have my wits about me, but maybe you should ask somebody else,' commented a jovial Chief Justice Alexander in a recent media interview.

Lee Strang, an associate law professor at the University of Toledo College of Law, supports a mandatory retirement age for Supreme Court justices, stating:

> It's not unjust to take into account the age of folks who are doing this very heavy intellectual lifting. These are not easy jobs; it takes a lot of intellectual firepower to do them.

But Howard Eglit, a law professor at Chicago-Kent College of Law, disagrees, claiming that age-limit laws were enacted in many states 'based in good measure on the assumption that increasing age carries with it declining intellectual ability'. Professor Eglit states that he opposes such a reform because:

> It's an inflexible rule which is harsh in one respect because it weeds out both the competent and the incompetent. I think you should judge people on the basis of competency, how they're performing, not on the basis of age. Age is an individualised thing. You can have a 60-year-old who's suffering from dementia, and a 90-year-old who's doing just fine.

Former New York state Chief Judge Judith Kaye, who was forced out of office by that state's age-limit law after she turned 70 in 2008, said she would not have left the 'dream of a lifetime' job if she had not had to, but stopped short in an interview of directly criticising her state's mandatory retirement law, saying she had 'mixed emotions' about it. But the former chief judge did not go home to retirement. She is now an attorney at a leading law firm in New York City. And in his media interview, Chief Justice Alexander said that after stepping down from Washington state's highest court in 2011, he was considering a return to the state appeal court where he began his judicial career at the age of 37. After retirement, judges in Washington state can act as pro tem judges, filling in as a substitute judge in any of the state's courts.

One further point needs to be made about these proposed reforms. One reason why the reforms were proposed concerned the significant increase in life expectancy in the United States. The point is made that whereas in 1900 the life expectancy for a white male was just 48, by 2000 it was 75. But that is life expectancy *at birth*, and justices of the Supreme Court are not appointed at birth. Even a century and more ago, once one had survived infancy and childhood, life expectancy was not that different to what it is today. For example, the life expectancy of a 70-year-old in 1900 was a further 9 years; in 2000 it was only a further 13 years. So the life expectancy argument is, to put it mildly, somewhat misleading.

But the most significant negative of both these reforms — a fixed 18-year term and a mandatory retirement age — is that because both of them would require a constitutional amendment, the chances of them happening are nil. Life tenure for Supreme Court justices is not a doorstep issue that is exciting ordinary voters. Indeed, some would argue that it is a non-issue, and that these proposals are solutions looking for a problem. The current system works perfectly well.

Elected justices?

But finally we turn to the most radical reform, to replace appointment of justices by election. Of course, this reform could run alongside both term limits and a mandatory retirement age. Chief Justice Gerry Alexander of Washington state, to whom we referred above, was first elected to that state's highest court in 1994 and was re-elected in 2000 and 2006. In 2011 he was being forced to retire 5 years into his third 6-year term.

Table 6.4 and Figure 6.2 show that 21 states, including Illinois, Michigan, Ohio and Texas, elect all of their state judges including those to their highest court. North Dakota also elects its Supreme Court judges. Seven of these 22 states, including Illinois and Texas, hold partisan elections for their highest

Table 6.4   Selection methods for state judges

Selection method	Supreme Court	Appeal courts*	Trial courts**
Election (partisan)	7	6	12
Election (non-partisan)	15	12	21
Total	**22**	**18**	**33**
Appointment	17	16	11
Appointment with state commission	9	4	6
Total	**26**	**20**	**17**
Indirect election	2	2	2
Assigned	0	1	0

*Figures in this column add up to 41 as 9 states do not have separate appeal courts.

**Figures in this column add up to 52 as Kansas and Maryland use both election and appointment to their trial courts.

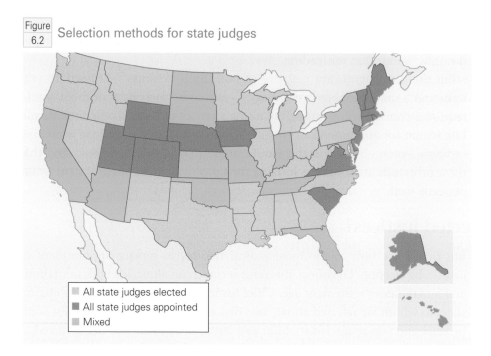

Figure 6.2 Selection methods for state judges

- All state judges elected
- All state judges appointed
- Mixed

court; the remaining 15 states, including Michigan and Ohio, hold non-partisan elections. A further 11 states elect some of their judges, thus a total of 33 of the 50 states have elected judges at some or all levels of the state judiciary. So a suggestion to elect federal judges cannot entirely be ruled out of court, so to speak.

The proposal to elect justices of the Supreme Court comes principally from those who see the current Court as lacking in democratic accountability for an institution which, as we have seen, exercises significant political power. The argument continues that because the confirmation process has been turned largely into a circus, impeachment is virtually unused, and the justices enjoy life tenure without any form of recall process, therefore the Supreme Court suffers from a significant democratic deficit which election, it is claimed, would correct. But would it? If the election of state judges is anything to go by, intro-ducing elections for justices of the Supreme Court could raise more problems than it solves. There are a number of problems that have arisen with regard to state judicial elections.

First, elections are based on the dubious premise that the voters are attentive, well informed about the candidates and knowledgeable about the requirements of the office. In fact, in state judicial elections, the voters appear inattentive, uninformed about the candidate and largely ignorant of what is required to be a competent and fair judge. State judicial elections are usually issueless and have lower voter participation rates than those for the state legislature or state executive positions. Most incumbents are easily re-elected and often run unopposed.

Second, elections may discourage well-qualified people from seeking judicial office. According to Jona Goldschmidt of the University of Miami Law School, 'many attorneys have a philosophical distaste for politics and political campaigning, and thus refrain from seeking [elective judicial] office'. Although one could quite imagine Associate Justice Antonin Scalia rather enjoying the rough and tumble of an election campaign, one could certainly not say the same of the likes of Anthony Kennedy or Ruth Bader Ginsburg.

Third, elections could well compromise judicial independence. Judges, unlike other elected officials, should not be governed by the transient whims of public opinion, which are likely to vote an unpopular, although competent, judge out of office for rendering plausible but nonetheless controversial decisions. How would a Supreme Court justice fare who decided that burning the American flag is a First Amendment protected right or that the death penalty contravenes the Eighth Amendment's ban on 'cruel punishments'?

Fourth, there would be the inevitable issue of campaign finance: how to deal with problems associated with judges who must campaign and seek campaign contributions, while still getting the Court's business accomplished during election time. Such problems are already in evidence in the state judicial elections. In his biennial State of the Judiciary speech to a joint session of the state legislature in February 2009, Texas Chief Justice Wallace Jefferson reserved the bulk of his speech to address what he described as 'the corrosive influence of money' in judicial elections. Polls show that more than 80% of Texans believe that campaign contributions to state judges influence courtroom decisions. 'That's an alarming figure — four out of five,' stated Chief Justice Jefferson. 'If the public believes that judges are biased towards contributors then confidence in our courts will suffer.' He asked the state legislature to amend the Texas Constitution to replace judicial elections with a merit selection system. In 1994, judicial candidates across the 33 states which use elections for their state judiciaries raised a total of $20.7 million; by 2004 that figure had more than doubled. Two candidates competing for a seat on the Illinois Supreme Court in 2004 raised a remarkable $9.3 million, breaking all records for fundraising in state judicial races.

Writing in the September 2002 issue of *Nation* magazine, Michael Scherer made some chilling comments about state judicial elections which one could easily translate on to the national level were US Supreme Court justices to be elected:

> The flood of money is driven by a fierce battle over judicial philosophy that has pitted trial lawyers, consumer advocates and unions against corporations, their attorneys and their trade associations.

James Sample of the Brennan Center for Justice at New York University likewise concludes that:

> The dramatic increase in the role of special interest spending creates a perception that judges are accountable to particular constituencies rather than to the rule of law.

In the light of all this, it is hardly surprising that in December 2009 the recently retired former Supreme Court Justice Sandra Day O'Connor gave her name to a new nationwide initiative to replace state judicial elections with merit selection. O'Connor stated:

> This initiative is a matter of great importance to our country. The amount of money poured into judicial campaigns has skyrocketed, intensifying the need to re-examine how we choose judges in America. I believe it is our moral duty and obligation to restore the public's confidence in our judicial system.

This would seem a strange moment then to advocate the election of justices to the United States Supreme Court. If one believes, as many do, that even the current merit-based selection and confirmation process for Supreme Court justices is overly politicised, too much influenced by interest groups and the media, then it is likely that such concerns would merely be magnified were elections to such posts to be introduced. That is certainly the experience of the individual states.

Conclusion

We have seen both in this and in other chapters that the nomination and confirmation process for Supreme Court justices is open to significant criticism. The Founding Fathers believed — in the late eighteenth century — that all federal judges, including Supreme Court justices, should be appointed for life. But then they also believed in a lot of other things which were written into the Constitution — an appointed Senate, slavery and a male-only electorate, to name but a few. But the Senate is now directly elected, slavery was abolished and women got the vote. Is appointment for life still right for Supreme Court justices, or should it go the way of those other anachronisms just mentioned?

In this chapter we have raised various problems associated with life tenure: justices serving much longer than the Founding Fathers would have envisaged; vacancies occurring at irregular and longer intervals; problems associated with senility; the failure of the impeachment process to be used as an effective check on the Court; and the Court's lack of democratic accountability in an era when its political importance has significantly increased. These problems could be corrected through either one or a combination of reforms, including a fixed 18-year term, a mandatory retirement age, or election. But these reforms would bring with them other significant drawbacks. They would also all require the passing of a constitutional amendment. This makes reform highly problematic and unlikely. Surely a better way forward would be to try to correct those specific weaknesses of the nomination and confirmation process that we identified in the opening chapter. It is also worth remembering that of the three institutions of the federal government — Congress, the president and the Supreme Court — it is the Supreme Court that is regularly held in the highest esteem by the public. Alexander Hamilton, writing in *The Federalist* number 78 in the summer of 1788, said this:

> Whoever attentively considers the different departments of power must perceive, that, in a government in which they are separated from each other, the judiciary, from the nature of its functions, will always be the least dangerous to the political rights of the Constitution; because it will be least in a capacity to annoy or injure them.

Not only may the Supreme Court be part of 'the least dangerous branch', it may also be in the least need of radical reform. Bert Lance, a Georgia businessman who served as President Carter's Budget Director in the late 1970s, once remarked:

> Any attempt to improve on a system that already works is pointless and may even be detrimental.

This was quoted in the May 1977 issue of *Nation's Business* in its popularised form: 'If it ain't broke don't fix it.' On this, at least, Bert Lance was correct.

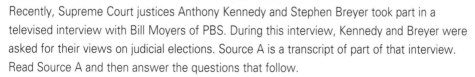

Task 6.1

Recently, Supreme Court justices Anthony Kennedy and Stephen Breyer took part in a televised interview with Bill Moyers of PBS. During this interview, Kennedy and Breyer were asked for their views on judicial elections. Source A is a transcript of part of that interview. Read Source A and then answer the questions that follow.

Task 6.1 (continued)

Source A

BREYER: In the confirmation process, I sat for 17 hours in front of the Senate Judiciary Committee. And they asked me questions I had to answer. And it was on television. If [people round the country] were watching and listening, and they decided they didn't like what they saw they might communicate with their elected representatives. And perhaps I wouldn't have been confirmed. Well what do I think about that? I thought that that was an effort to inject a popular element, a democratic element into the selection of a person who, once he is selected and confirmed, is beyond electoral control. Now why do we have such a system? Because, on the one hand, people want judges to be independent. Nobody wants a judge to be subject to the political whim of the moment. At the same time, we live in a democracy, and for that reason I think it is appropriate to have some element of public control. And that element of public control in the federal system is introduced through the selection process and the confirmation process.

MOYERS: The concern that both of you have expressed is in particular about campaign contributions to state judicial races. Why do you see that as a threat to independence and neutrality?

KENNEDY: Well, in part, it's because the campaign process itself does not easily adapt to judicial selection. Democracy is raucous, hurly-burly, rough-and-tumble. This is a difficult world for a judge, a scholarly, detached, neutral person to operate within. And when you add the component of this mad scramble to raise money and to spend money, it becomes even worse for the obvious reason that we're concerned that there will be either the perception or the reality that judicial independence is undermined.

MOYERS: We actually talked to a lobbyist in Texas on the record, on camera. He's a lobbyist for the Texas Medical Association and he boasted that he had succeeded in reshaping the philosophy of the Texas Supreme Court through an all-out political campaign and very large donations. They took [control of the Court] from the trial lawyers who had been making contributions and had influenced the Court on the other side of the aisle. What does that say about judicial independence?

BREYER: I think it shows that if you have one group of people doing it, you'll get another group of people doing it. And if you have A contributing to affect a court one way, you'll have B trying to affect it the other way and pretty soon you'll have a clash of political interests. Now, that's fine for a legislature. But if you have that in the court system, you will then destroy confidence that the judges are deciding things on merit.

(a) How does Justice Breyer think that the confirmation process is a democratic check on the Court?

(b) Why does Justice Kennedy think that judges and elections are somewhat incompatible?

(c) Why does Justice Breyer have concerns about fund raising in judicial elections?

Guidance

(a) You will find the material in the first Breyer extract.

(b) Look at the adjectives that Kennedy uses to describe both the campaign process and judges: think why these will not easily be compatible.

(c) Look at both Bill Moyers' question and Breyer's response.